# She Writes for Him

## Stories of Resilient Faith

# She Writes for Him

## Stories of Resilient Faith

ROMANS 8:28
BOOKS

AN IMPRINT OF REDEMPTION PRESS

FEATURING BEST-SELLING AUTHORS

Carol Kent
Tammy Trent
Dr. Saundra Dalton-Smith

Published by Romans 8:28 Books, an imprint of Redemption Press,
PO Box 427, Enumclaw, WA 98022
Toll Free (844) 2REDEEM (273-3336)

Redemption Press is honored to present this title in partnership with the author. Redemption Press provides our imprint seal representing design excellence, creative content, and high-quality production.

"Why Do I Feel This Way?" excerpt from *Unlocked: 5 Myths Holding Your Influence Captive*, © 2013 by Cynthia Cavanaugh. Published by New Hope Publishers, Birmingham, Alabama. NewHopePublishers.com. Reprinted by permission.

"The Day the World Changed" was compiled from two books by Tammy Trent: *Beyond the Sorrow* (2015) and *Learning to Breathe Again* (2006), both published by Thomas Nelson. Used with permission.

"Dare to Forgive" excerpt from *Anchored: Leading Through the Storms*, © 2018 by Cynthia Cavanaugh. Published by New Hope Publishers, Birmingham, Alabama. NewHopePublishers.com. Reprinted by permission.

"The Truth that Sets You Free," excerpt from *Planned from the Start*, © 2019 by Lorraine Marie Varela. Published by Romans 8:28 Books, an imprint of Redemption Press, PO Box 427, Enumclaw, WA 98022. Reprinted by permission.

Permissions for the Bible versions used are listed at the end of the book.

ISBN 13 HC: 978-1-7329625-9-0
ISBN 13 Mobi: 978-1-951310-04-2
ISBN 13 ePub: 978-1-951310-05-9

Library of Congress Catalog Card Number: 2020931351

# Dedication

This debut edition of *She Writes for Him* is dedicated to women, near and far, who've been silenced by the enemy. It's time to seek the healing we need and grow in the grace only Jesus can provide.

Athena Dean Holtz, Publisher

# TABLE OF CONTENTS

## She Writes for Him
### Stories of Resilient Faith

# Part 2: *Loss*

# Part 3: *Abortion*

# Part 4: *Depression and Anxiety*

# Part 5: Betrayal

# Your Story Truly Matters

In the past decade, the phrase "Your story matters" has bounced around the internet on memes, blogs, and social media posts. We are a generation who is capturing the value of recording the narrative of our life experiences. This is nothing new. Before the written word was available to the average human, stories were passed on to preserve memories. Fathers gathered children and grandchildren to tell tales of milestone events. Heroes grew into legends as stories were relayed over generations. Inspiration was birthed as retelling of momentous circumstances motivated people to rise up and follow in the footsteps of courageous men and women.

The Bible recounts events from Moses to Nehemiah in the Old Testament to Jesus and Paul in the New Testament. Their voices teach us to engage our creator God in deeper intimacy. The stories rooted in God's truth with the Holy Spirit lead us toward transformation and encourage us to embrace our individual stories. Our narrative becomes a catalyst of influence to make God famous to serve and inspire others.

The authors in this book have experienced the kind of hardship that has pushed them desperately into the arms of Jesus. With God's help they not only have recovered but have gone beyond the label of an overcomer and stand as a resilient witnesses to God's glory.

*She Writes for Him: Resilient Stories of Faith* is our debut in a series of volumes meant to showcase ordinary people whose stories are noble journeys of God's healing, redemptive grace.

In this first volume, our goal is to address hot-burner topics that are facing the church and Christian community. Issues that can't be ignored and yet need authentic voices to lead the way with godly truth.

Our prayer is you will find in this collection an example, phrase, or challenge to help you on your journey. May these stories infuse hope for your life and give you the courage to tell your beautiful story—because as they say, "Your story matters."

## Cynthia Cavanaugh
**Managing Editor**

# Part 1

# Shame

## Chapter One

# Facing the Unthinkable
### Carol Kent

The phone rang in the middle of the night, waking me from a deep sleep. Still dazed, I saw my husband pick up the receiver, then watched as a look of shock and disbelief covered his face. With tears spilling onto his cheeks, he looked at me and said, "Jason has just been arrested for the murder of his wife's first husband. He's in the jail in Orlando."

I had never been in shock before. First came extreme nausea. I slipped out of bed, but my legs wouldn't hold my weight. Thoughts swirled in my head. *Our son is a graduate of the US Naval Academy. He's a husband and a stepfather to two little girls. He's never been in trouble before. I must be in the middle of a dreadful nightmare. I'll soon wake up and find out that this is just a bad dream.*

But as night turned to morning, the facts were confirmed. Our son had pulled a trigger in a public parking lot, and a man had died. Gene and I reviewed our recollections of Jason's phone calls during the past year. We noted that instead of talking about his work with the navy, global concerns, or recent news, he was obsessed with fear for the safety of his stepdaughters. There were multiple allegations of abuse against their biological father, and it appeared he would soon get unsupervised visits with them.

> For the first time in my adult life, I felt powerless, exposed, and afraid of what others would think of me and of our family.

Jason's first military assignment outside of the continental US was Hawaii, and that would mean the girls might have as much as six weeks of visitation time with their father during the summer. In retrospect, we saw that Jason began unraveling—mentally, emotionally, and spiritually—as he fixated on his fears for what might happen to the girls. And now our twenty-five-year-old son had done the unthinkable. He'd shot and killed his wife's first husband.

Only two weeks earlier, Gene and I had walked together along the Saint Clair River in Port Huron, Michigan, where we lived. The trees were dressed in their multicolored regalia, sporting their brilliant bursts of red, yellow, and orange. It had been a sunny day, and the temperature was brisk. We'd talked about the new season of life we were in with a grown son, a daughter-in-law, and two precocious stepgranddaughters. We were traveling internationally, as I spoke at Christian retreats and conferences, and Gene had become the chief operating officer of the ministry, managing the business part of our work and handling travel arrangements. I'd looked up at my husband and said, "Does life get any better than this?"

Over the next few days, weeks, and months, everything changed. Thoughts swirled and emotions of fear, shock, and panic consumed us. We grieved for the family of the deceased. We were afraid for our son's safety. He was brutally beaten in the jail two weeks after his arrest, which resulted in his two front teeth being broken off. I turned inward instead of reaching out to friends.

An emotion that I didn't have much experience with consumed me—shame. I wondered what I had done wrong as a parent that would propel my son into making such a devastating choice. I experienced an unpleasant self-consciousness accompanied with a negative evaluation of myself. I felt like withdrawing from people and shrugged away from answering the phone or from responding to communications from well-meaning friends. For the first time in my adult life, I felt powerless, exposed, and afraid of what others would think of me and of our family. Mistrust of people thrust me into retreating from my usual gregarious connections with others. I wanted to hide.

As the oldest of six preacher's kids, I was used to being in the public eye, and I had volunteered for leadership in a myriad of roles both in and out of my local church. After I married and eventually became a Christian speaker and author, my life was filled with interacting with large numbers of people.

But now I was the mother of a murderer.

*Would anyone want me to speak at their event? How would we pay for our son's legal expenses if we left the ministry? Would people assume poor parenting was the cause of our son's devastating choice?* My immediate assumption was that Gene and I would have a major loss of reputation, in addition to dealing with the extreme fears for our son's safety.

The lies of the Enemy were taunting me:

- *If you had been a more involved mother, this would not have happened.*
- *If you had read your Bible more often and prayed more fervently, your son wouldn't have committed this crime.*
- *If you had been less busy, you would have seen the danger signs and fixed this problem before a man was murdered.*

I blamed myself for what had happened, which triggered more shame. My son was already repentant for his sin and well aware of the fact that he had made an idol out of his own ability to protect his stepdaughters instead of trusting in God to be their protector and teaching them to run and scream for help. But the Enemy convinced me that I was the cause of my son's action.

Shame is often brought about by our own wrong choices that result in ungodly behavior or because of a sinful act committed against us. For instance, a victim of sexual assault sometimes feels more shame than the perpetrator. Remember the biblical story of Tamar, who was raped by her brother Amnon? He expelled her and said he wanted nothing to do with her. She walked away mourning, enveloped in shame. Second Samuel describes her exit: "And Tamar put ashes on her head and tore the long robe that she wore. And she laid her hand on her head and went away, crying aloud as she went" (2 Samuel 13:19 ESV). Not only are we capable of feeling shame for what we've done, we often experience false shame over what's been done to us. This results in unwarranted and sometimes irrational feelings of inadequacy, unworthiness, and self-doubt.

When I was able to think clearly, I knew I had been a good mother. I recognized that I had led my son to a personal faith relationship with Christ and that my husband and I had provided a positive, Christ-centered home environment—but there were still days when I had trouble believing that truth.

Shame has plagued us since Adam and Eve bit into the fruit and saw their nakedness. Their first instinct was to hide—from each other and from God (Genesis 3:7–11). No surprise there! They now stood guilty before God and were vulnerable to each other and to Satan. Today we live in a sinful world and have the same instinct to hide ourselves. The kind of shame we often experience is a combination of failure and pride. We fail morally (sin), we fail due to our limitations (weakness), and we fail because the whole creation doesn't work right (Romans 8:20). When we know we don't live up to the expectations of others, because of our pride we're ashamed of our failures and weaknesses.

Often we'll go to any length to hide from others. For a while I hid in my home— not wanting to face the people in my church or in my community who had now read about my son's arrest for murder in our local paper. Sometimes we hide in perfectionism and workaholism. We hide on the internet by filling our minds with videos, movies, and music to drown out the emotional pain of our shame. It's possible to hide behind humor and through extroversion and introversion—through anything that allows us to keep conversation on the surface rather than by being vulnerable and real with the people around us.

The key to breaking shame's power is in the refuge of Jesus Christ. His death and resurrection provide the only remedy for the shame we feel over our sin failures (Hebrews 9:26). My son has discovered this truth. The key to breaking the power of my own pride-fueled shame was through fully embracing the power of the humility-fueled faith in the work of Christ and His promises. Shame says, "You're guilty! You failed! You're lacking!" But Jesus pronounces us "Guiltless!" He promises that His grace will be sufficient for us in all our weaknesses (2 Corinthians 12:9–10).

Consider the woman at the well. Her life was in shambles. After five failed marriages, she wanted to hide from the comments, the whispers, and the stares from those who looked at her with judgmental eyes. She went to the well when the sun was blazing so she could draw water alone (John 4). That day her life changed because she listened to Jesus and believed in Him. Her life was redeemed and her shame destroyed. He

can do that for you, too. Tell Him what has triggered your shame. Believe that "God will supply every need of yours according to his riches in glory in Christ Jesus" (Philippians 4:19 ESV).

## Resilient Truth

There is therefore now no condemnation for those who are in Christ Jesus. For the law of the Spirit of life has set you free in Christ Jesus from the law of sin and death. (Romans 8:1–2 ESV)

## Resilient Prayer

*Father in heaven*, You are my Savior, my hope, my strength, and my safe place. You are the God to whom nothing is impossible. In the middle of my difficult situation, I'm tempted to take on all of the responsibility for the wrong choices of those closest to me. My natural inclination is to run from people and places where I might find judgmental eyes or hear critical remarks. Help me to confess any known sin, and then declare that the false accusations of others and those I place upon myself are not from You. I reject them and give them no place in my heart. I know I have been forgiven. Help me to reject shameful feelings because they are not from You. I'm fixing my heart on following Jesus and living in the victory He won for me on the cross.

 *Resilient Action*

In what area of your life do you feel shame? Is there a sin to confess, or are you allowing yourself to be judged because of the wrongdoing of a family member? Talk to God, using the prayer above, and then make a list of who God says you are. (I'll help you start your list.)

- I'm made in the image of God. (Genesis 1:27)
- I am fearfully and wonderfully made. (Psalm 139:14)
- I am forgiven. (1 John 1:9)
- I am not condemned by God. (Romans 8:1–2)
- I am loved with an everlasting love. (Jeremiah 31:3)

Carol Kent is a bestselling author and an international speaker. She's the executive director of the Speak Up Conference, a ministry committed to helping Christians develop their speaking and writing skills. She and her husband founded the nonprofit organization Speak Up for Hope, which benefits inmates and their families. She's the author of over twenty-five books, including *When I Lay My Isaac Down*, *Becoming a Woman of Influence*, and *He Holds My Hand*. Visit Carol at www.carolkent.org.

Chapter Two

## Unveiling Shame
### Dawn Scott Damon

Someone once said, "Guilt is when you feel like you've done something wrong. Shame is when you believe you *are* something wrong."

That definition describes the distinctions between the two emotions well. At one time I was filled with both feelings of shame and guilt.

I don't have total recall of my abuse; however, my vivid memories tell me with certainty that I was sexually molested as a child. I can't tell you when it began or how many years it lasted. Until a few years ago, I couldn't even have told you how my abuse affected me.

But I can tell you who the perpetrator was—my dad by day and my abuser by night.

His practice was predictable. He would quietly enter my room. The smell of his alcohol-laden breath permeated the air as he crawled between my twin sheets. I would freeze.

*Pretend to be asleep and it will be over soon.*

I always acted unaware of what was happening. My pseudo-comatose state became my only defense against him. I couldn't bear to acknowledge his presence—that was far too horrifying to consider.

I suppose it was early on when thoughts and fears overwhelmed me and questions flooded my mind.

*Why is he doing this?*

*What have I done to make him think this is okay?*

*Where's my mom?*

But soon silence replaced unanswered questions, and I learned to lay silent and numb. Playing dead became natural.

*Don't move.*

*Don't breathe.*

*Don't cry.*

*Don't feel.*

## Unveiling Shame

Over the next few years, *Don't cry; Don't feel* became my way of surviving. My head became disconnected from my heart. Instead of enjoying the remarkable kaleidoscope of teenage emotions, I morphed into a more dignified form of numb. Stoicism.

*Keep your emotions on lockdown, Dawn. No one likes a crybaby.*

I appeared strong, but I was a house of glass.

My biggest struggle was guilt about my response to the sexual assault. I didn't understand why I didn't do anything to stop the abuse. My inner prosecuting attorney tormented me with finely crafted accusations.

*So, Dawn, you say your abuse was awful. Hmmm, okay, but did you ever tell anyone? Did you ever scream for help or yell to make him stop? At the very least, did you ever say no?*

*No, I didn't,* I'd tell myself.

*Then you're GUILTY! It's your fault.*

Over and over again I condemned myself as guilty and worthy of the sentence—a life without joy, purpose, or freedom.

Sexual abuse stole my innocence, and I was left feeling . . . *nothing*, nothing but shame.

I didn't recognize it at first, but these feelings of humiliation and inner distress forced me into the shadows. I hid and covered my true essence under shame's veil. My fear was illogical, but exposing my inner self was frightening.

Decide to believe God and His Word. He wants to peel shame off you and reveal to you the beauty of who you truly are.

I unconsciously reasoned, *I can't let anyone see who I really am because who I am is unacceptable and bad. If I let you see who I am, you won't like me. Ha! I don't even like me.*

The voice of shame debilitated me and overshadowed my potential. *You're defective, flawed, a disgrace*, it whispered. The voice convinced me I didn't just *do* something bad, I *was* something bad.

Shameful.

Satan wants to destroy our lives, and he effectively uses shame to accomplish his goal. In Revelation 12:10 Satan is called the accuser of Christians. As a young believer, when I discovered that verse, my eyes were opened. Through the revelation of the Holy Spirit, I saw that the voice verbally accosting me all these years didn't originate from me and certainly not from God. It was from Satan.

Does an inner prosecuting attorney berate you? You can be assured that the source of the voice is the devil, telling you you're defective and unworthy. Satan tries to shame you, and he speaks his native language of lies. Jesus stated in John 8:44 that Satan is a master deceiver and no truth can be found in him. When he speaks, the essence of his true character is heard through the malicious lies he tells you—and there are many, for he is the Father of Lies. Instead of believing his devious words, pay attention to the clashing dissonance between what you read in God's Word and the condemnation you feel in your soul. Decide to believe God and His Word. He wants to peel shame off you and reveal to you the beauty of who you truly are. Are you ready to trust Him?

## To Know and Be Known

I wanted to be known, but shame kept me at a distance. I longed for intimacy, but I covered myself for safety, embarrassed by my need. Still, I wondered what it must be like to be fully known by someone who loved me. I'd been told I had to take the risk if I was ever going to be done with shame. I thought about the courage of King David, who intentionally invited the all-seeing God into his life. "Search me, God, and know my heart; test me and know my anxious thoughts. See if there is any offensive way in me, and lead me in the way everlasting" (Psalm 139:23–24 NIV).

*See . . . me.*

So I cried out to God, "I want to be known by You, Lord! I don't want to be invisible anymore. I want to come out of the shadows and experience your love."

Today I believe one of the most beautiful experiences of my life, and Yours too, is found in intimacy—"to know and to be known." I also believe that longing for closeness is not wrong; in fact, it's from God. As human beings, our creator God designed and wired us to enjoy transparency and closeness with each other—to be fully known and *feel no shame*, and to fully know and *have no judgments*. Only in this close and intimate bond of acceptance do we experience the true fullness of joy that God desires for us.

But sin messes up our joy and intimacy.

One fateful day in the Garden of Eden, Satan crept in and beguiled the humans (Genesis 3). Man and woman succumbed to his deception, and in one nibble of the forbidden fruit, the guilty pair forfeited their purity and freedom. Shame quickly filled the void as the man and woman ran for cover to conceal their true selves. They hid from the eyes of God. They hid from one another. Innocence was gone, and shame was born. This is what happened to us.

But our human desire did not change, only our fear. We still long for love. We're created with a desire to be known and accepted for who we truly are. Yet we deflect the very intimacy we crave. We despise the eyes that behold us—the gaze that wants to know us. We run for cover, fearing to our very core the prospect of being exposed, while our faces flush with the fire of shame. Such is the fear of "in-to-me-see" (intimacy).

Shame cannot live in the presence of God's love. For shame at its root is fear of exposure. And perfect love casts out all fear.

Back to Psalm 139, where we glimpse an amazing conversation that at first blush could set off a bomb inside a terrified survivor. We hear David's heart cry, *See me! Know me!* This psalmist's raw, intrinsic soul longing burned like fire in his belly. In essence he begged, *Lord, let Your eyes search me. Let Your eyes see into the depth of my being. I need You to come close. I want no secrets with You, God. I long to have Your attention. I want to be known by You.*

Wow!

Today I renounce shame and refuse to allow it to cover me. I throw off toxic shame and false guilt and declare I am free. My head is held high because of Your redeeming love, Jesus, and I am radiant.

How many of us would welcome, actually *invite* a spiritual search from an all-powerful God? But that's exactly my point. David found the secret to ending shame in his life—friendship with God. When he met God, he met love. Grace. Mercy. Acceptance.

David, known as a man after God's own heart, felt comfortable with God's eyes searching him (Acts 13:22). And after that search? David saw himself just as God saw him. Read the words of David: "I praise you because I am fearfully and wonderfully made; your works are wonderful, I know that full well" (Psalm 139:14 NIV). Shame cannot live in the presence of God's love. For shame at its root is fear of exposure. And perfect love casts out all fear. God is safe. He sees you and He loves you. He'll put an end to the shame that is stealing from you.

*Resilient Truth*

Those who look to him are radiant; their faces are never covered with shame. (Psalm 34:5 NIV)

## Resilient Prayer

*Lord*, sometimes shame overtakes me, and I feel small, unworthy, and embarrassed. Lies tell me I am unloved. I want to hide myself from You and others. But today I renounce shame and refuse to allow it to cover me. I throw off toxic shame and false guilt and declare I am free. My head is held high because of Your redeeming love, Jesus, and I am radiant. I face each day with joy, knowing I will do my best and leave the rest to You. In Jesus's name!

## Resilient Action

In what ways has shame caused you to hide and cover your true self? Has Satan lied to you about your worth and value? Next time you hear that accusing voice, name some ways you will take steps to defeat it.

Dawn Scott Damon is an award-winning author, speaker, singer/songwriter, and freedom coach. An ordained minister, Dawn is the lead pastor of Tribes, a multiethnic church in Grand Rapids, Michigan. The founder of the FreedomGirl Sisterhood Conference and Radio Broadcast, she blogs at freedomgirlsisterhood.com. Dawn and her husband, Paul, have five children and eleven grandchildren. They live in Rockford, Michigan.

## Chapter Three

## Hidden beneath the Surface
### Nikki Godsil

Feeling confident and prepared, I stepped onto the bus with the rest of my cheerleading squad. I stayed up all night, practiced every move to every cheer in my new bedroom. We had just moved from Virginia to Pennsylvania, and I was terrified of middle school. I honestly couldn't have cared less about cheering, being a bit of a tomboy, but I was willing to look past the pom-poms in exchange for friendship. With my starched blue-and-gold vest, perfectly pleated skirt, and carefully curled hair, I walked through the aisle to find a seat. A long, bony finger pricked my chest, stopping me.

"What is this?" Coach said.

"I'm sorry. What?" I managed to mutter through the golf-ball-sized lump in my throat.

"You're wearing the wrong shirt. Guess you'll be sitting on the bench until you can get the simple things right."

It felt like every eyeball was staring at me, directly into my soul. All I heard were the whispers and shushed laughter around me. I forced the tears down as a wave of heat flushed over my face. My heart raced.

"I don't want to be on this stupid squad anyway," I yelled as I forced her hand away and stomped off the bus.

It sent shockwaves of pain every time I pictured that forceful finger in my face, so I promised myself I'd never have to endure that again. Pretending became my friend, and hiding became my safe place.

Fast-forward years later, and life felt disconnected. My external life didn't match the internal. How could I feel so unfulfilled when I had everything I worked so hard for: a husband, four healthy kids, a career as an RN? Yet the external fulfillment masked my internal yearning for more. I was ashamed to admit the emptiness I felt, in fear people would think I was ungrateful.

The reality was, my marriage was failing, my career was taxing, and my kids drained me more than they gave me joy—and this disconnect was making me miserable. I was drowning in my self-made life. Shame told me to pretend I was happy because I didn't deserve anything more than what I had and that to desire anything more was wrong. To voice my internal pain raised the questions, "What's the purpose?" and "What will people think?" Shame told me to pretend I was fine, to guard my heart from feeling the pangs of rejection like I did that day on the bus.

Unfortunately, pretending also guarded me from feeling the benefits of genuine and authentic relationships with both others and the One who could heal the wound of rejection. The very thing I thought protected me from more harm was the thing that kept me from healing.

I believed resurfacing the pain of the past would unravel the life I'd worked so hard to achieve. Pretending everything was fine became the answer to my pain. Vulnerability became my sworn enemy.

The problem with avoiding pain isn't that we can't function—it's that it keeps reappearing when we try and move forward. A string of days goes by, and everything seems to be going well. Then you wake up, and the pain of your past shifts you back to the ache you worked so hard to forget. Before you know it, you're stuck in this unhealthy cycle of lies, living a life where worth is defined by the opinions of others. You're exhausted, lonely, and unable to reveal your genuine, authentic self, in fear

> The very thing I thought protected me from more harm was the thing that kept me from healing.

of being hurt again. Shame says your brokenness is your cross to bear, but Jesus says it's His.

For God to begin to make beauty out of the ashes of shame, we have to admit self-sufficiency

There's no wound too small, too big, or too insignificant for Him to heal. Your story matters to Him, and He wants to hear it.

isn't enough. Numbing the pain only gives it room to grow. It's the acknowledgement and bringing it into light that shame finally loosens its grip on life. As we humble ourselves before the Lord, the deceit that drapes over us like a blanket slowly lifts. Talking about the pain births new hope for fulfillment and purpose.

Haven't we all been here, friend? As Christians we often believe we have to put on our best self to be worthy of acceptance and love. So we struggle with shame in isolation. Today I want to invite you to feed your faith by revealing the truth about who you are in Christ. For it's in our true identity in Him we can break free from the lies of shame.

The path to healing begins by recognizing you're not alone. We live in a fallen world, where no one escapes trauma or sin. There's no wound too small, too big, or too insignificant for Him to heal. Your story matters to Him, and He wants to hear it.

Evidence of shame first entered the world in Genesis 3:7–8, where it says, "Then the eyes of both were opened, and they knew that they were naked. And they sewed fig leaves together and made themselves loincloths. And they heard the sound of the Lord God walking in the garden in the cool of the day, and the man and his wife hid themselves from the presence of the Lord God among the trees of the garden" (ESV).

When shame takes root in the fertile soil of our soul, it destroys the very make-up of who we are. It tells us we aren't wanted by the God who created us. This is how shame grows, hiding in the dark, behind the sin it planted itself in.

However, in Genesis 3:21 it says, "And the Lord God made for Adam and for his wife garments of skins and clothed them" (ESV).

By clothing them, God demonstrated He would never leave us sitting in our shame but would cover us in the midst of it. What He didn't do was condemn,

What we need has
already been done.
Jesus has already
turned all shame
into glory.

reject, scold, or leave. His first response is to love.

God never says you aren't enough. Shame does. He never says you aren't loved, chosen, and accepted just as you are. Shame's deceit leads us to believe we're too broken to truly be loved and accepted just as we are.

The way to break free of our shame is by handing every broken, tattered, wounded portion of our soul over to Jesus.

A willingness to show our true self, no matter how dirty it is, requires vulnerability. Shame says vulnerability is weakness, but Jesus says it is your strength. It's in vulnerability we can present our most authentic, genuine selves to the one who can do the deepest work in our lives.

Isaiah 1:18–19 (ESV) says, "Though your sins are like scarlet, they shall be as white as snow; though they are red like crimson, they shall become like wool. If you are willing and obedient, you shall eat the good of the land."

Jesus wipes our sin away if we choose to let Him so we can eat the good of the land. The *land* in this verse is a prophetic statement referring to the restored Eden mentioned in Revelation 22:14. Our fulfillment and purpose is restored when we enter into a deep, connected relationship with the Lord again, eating of the fruit of His Spirit.

What we need has already been done. Jesus has already turned all shame into glory. When our identity is firmly rooted in Him, the opinions of this world no longer determine our worth. New life is waiting. All you have to do is choose to stand up, grab His hand, and let Him lift you out of the ash and into the light that promises redemption.

## ～ Resilient Truth

Take no part in the unfruitful works of darkness, but instead expose them. For it is shameful even to speak of the things that they do in secret. But when anything is exposed by the light, it becomes visible, for anything that becomes visible is light. Therefore it says, "Awake, O sleeper, and arise from the dead, and Christ will shine on you." (Ephesians 5:11–14 ESV)

## ～ Resilient Prayer

*Jesus, my Redeemer and Restorer,* I confess that I need You. Forgive me for believing the lies of the Enemy. I choose to praise You in the storm. Restore in me a spirit of hope, and build me into the oak of righteousness You've always intended me to be. I lay my robe at the foot of the cross, where Your blood washes every crimson stain away. I declare that I am made new, firmly planted in You.

I invite You in to heal the wounds of my past, remove the sin of shame that has festered in the darkness, and replace it with the fruits of Your spirit.

I boldly declare, from this day forward, to stand on the truth of Your Word. I invite the Holy Spirit to come in and search my heart. Help me grow into my new identity as a fully healed child of God, constantly seeking Your ways.

Help me grow into my new identity as a fully healed child of God, constantly seeking Your ways.

*Resilient Action*

What painful memory resurfaces when the Holy Spirit searches your heart? Write it below and tell the Lord your story. Speak the darkness into the light and begin the healing that leads to redemption and freedom.

_____

_____

_____

_____

_____

_____

_____

_____

_____

_____

_____

_____

_____

Nikki Godsil is a registered nurse, turned stay-at-home mama of four, turned writer. She is approachable, raw, and playfully witty, and she can take you from side-splitting laughter to tears of joy in the same sitting. You can find her at www.nikkigodsil.com, Instagram at @nlgodsil, or sitting around her sticky farmhouse table with friends.

Chapter Four

## When Life Experiences Define My Value
### Kristin Clouse

It happens to me at some of the most inopportune times: when I'm with a group of friends, driving down the road, watching a movie, talking with a loved one, or even shopping at the grocery store. Thoughts and memories of my past flood my soul and at times cause me to gasp for air.

I remember the details so clearly, as if it were yesterday.

*It's about six o'clock in the morning, and I am walking down the street. Tears are coming down my cheeks, but I feel numb and oblivious to what is around me. So many emotions are going through me at once, and I'm not sure what to do with what I'm feeling. I'm confused, scared, and relieved all at the same time. I'm angry at my friends who left me at the house, and I still can't believe they betrayed me that way. They said they would come back. I'd thought they would be right back, but they never came. Did they not realize what could happen to me?*

*"No," I think, they had no idea. "This can't be happening to me again."*

*They thought I was safe. I thought I was safe. These things don't happen to people we know. This can't be happening to me again. I try to catch my breath as I find the weight of the memories of sexual abuse threatening to come in like a tidal wave over me. I quickly put out of my mind those memories from a few years before. I can't allow those emotions to*

Although I stand in the
shower for longer than I
can recall, when I step out,
I notice I still felt dirty
and unclean. I wonder, Will
I ever feel clean again?

come tumbling out and mingle with the emotions I am now feeling. The words I am struggling to speak are taking form within my mind. I was held against my will, and I . . . was . . . raped.

As soon as I get home, I jump into the shower. As I stand with the water hitting my body, I wish the water could wash away what I'm feeling inside, but it doesn't. I'm not sure how long I stand there or how many tears I shed. The water and my tears blend together and fall off my body. My thoughts swirl around in my mind like the water swirling down the drain. What am I going to do? A voice inside my head repeatedly tells me that I need to tell my mom, but I'm afraid. I know what happened to me was wrong. It was dangerous, and I'm thankful to be alive. I can't believe I survived.

Although I stand in the shower for longer than I can recall, when I step out, I notice I still felt dirty and unclean. I wonder, Will I ever feel clean again?

It was in that moment shame came in and covered my soul like a dark, treacherous cloud.

Sadly, what I didn't realize then was I wouldn't feel clean for many years following this day. The trauma of this particular day propelled me into a life of feeling unclean, dirty, unwanted, unworthy, and shame filled. I was broken, damaged goods.

Shame had taken root within my soul when I was just fourteen years old. The experiences, the abuse that happened to me as a child and teen propelled me into a season of life where I believed it was my fault, I was to blame, and I was damaged goods.

Shame had become part of my identity.

In Genesis 3:10–11 we see the conversation between God and Adam after Adam and Eve ate of the forbidden fruit:

> They heard the sound of the Lord God walking in the garden
> at the time of the evening breeze, and the man and his wife hid

themselves from the presence of the Lord God among the trees of the garden. But the Lord God called to the man, and said to him, "Where are you?" He said, "I heard the sound of you in the garden, and I was afraid, because I was naked; and I hid myself." He said, "Who told you that you were naked? Have you eaten from the tree of which I commanded you not to eat?" (Genesis 3:8–11 NRSV)

The moment Adam and Eve ate of the apple, their thought processing and how they viewed themselves changed. Shame came in and made Adam and Eve ashamed of who they were. Shame came into their core belief of their identity and value, just as it did for me when I was fourteen years old.

Shame told me I was broken, unclean, unworthy, and unlovable. Over the years it has told me I am unqualified to be used by God. Have you heard these words as well? I thought so. The enemy of our soul wanted to shut me down and silence my voice. He is wanting to silence you too, my friend. The good news is, the power of shame in our lives can be broken.

Adam and Eve had always been naked in the garden; this was not something new. Every day they walked and talked with God and each other, and their nakedness was never an issue or thought. They were content with who they were and secure in their identities. They were children of God created to have a deep relationship with Him, and that is what they did day after day.

When they ate the apple, they consumed the lie that said they needed to be ashamed, embarrassed, and humiliated. Immediately, other thoughts invaded their minds: thoughts of worthlessness, unworthiness, and disdain. These thoughts, mindsets, or perceptions became a part of who they were, their identities, and out of shame they hid themselves from God.

What is shame whispering into your ear day after day?

Friends, I pray you hear this right now. God is the one from whom we should never hide. He is here for us right God is here to love, help, care for, and to walk with us into health and healing, allowing us to find our true identities once again.

> The power of shame was broken off of my life when I surrendered to God the broken pieces of my life. I invited Jesus into my story, my history, my pain, my shame, and God showed me there is no shame in our brokenness.

now to comfort and not to condemn us, blame us, or humiliate us. God is here to love, help, care for, and to walk with us into health and healing, allowing us to find our true identities once again. His heart is broken for us, and He is here to heal our hearts and help us get rid of shame once and for all.

Finally, shame is based on secrets. Adam and Eve hid themselves from God. They didn't want to tell Him what happened. They were embarrassed to face God and be in His presence. Fear and shame go hand in hand. The root of secret keeping is shame. It's not for our benefit or protection, it keeps us in bondage, and it blocks the healing process.

The power of shame was broken off of my life when I surrendered to God the broken pieces of my life. I invited Jesus into my story, my history, my pain, my shame, and God showed me there is *no shame in our brokenness!*

May those words resonate deep within each of us.

Through counseling, studying God's Word, and deep conversations with Jesus, I have learned my brokenness is not something I should fear or be ashamed of. Instead God has shown me that my brokenness is the very thing that He will use and is using for His glory. No longer do I cower in fear from the abuse I experienced. Even though at times the memories crash in on me like a six-foot wave, the power they once had on me is no longer there. Shame no longer has me bound up, and I have discovered who I am through Christ. Jesus has become the definer of my value, and I pray He will be for you as well.

Remember, there is no shame in our brokenness, and truly with Jesus, nothing or no one is beyond repair.

## ∾ Resilient Truth

Be strong and courageous. Do not be afraid; do not be discouraged, for the Lord your God will be with you wherever you go. (Joshua 1:9 NIV)

## ∾ Resilient Prayer

*Father*, help us to recognize shame and the lies it speaks into our lives every day. Give us courage as we face our fears, shame, and mistruths about our identity and value. Transform and renew our thinking so we may see ourselves the way You do. Lord, You created each of us with a specific purpose in mind, and we ask You to heal our souls so we can walk in the fullness of who You created us to be. Give us courage to face our past hurts and to invite You into our brokenness. In Jesus's name. Amen.

Heal our souls so we can walk in the fullness of who You created us to be. Give us courage to face our past hurts and to invite You into our brokenness.

*Resilient Action*

In what ways has shame defined your identity or value? What broken pieces of your life story do you need to give to God? Who is a safe person you can share your story with and break the power of secrecy?

_____

_____

_____

_____

_____

_____

_____

_____

_____

_____

_____

_____

_____

Kristin Clouse is a pastor, licensed counselor, speaker, mentor, founder of The Restore Movement for women, and published author of *Healing for Our Soul Gardens: Restoration and Wholeness after Sexual Abuse*. You can find her at www.KristinClouse.com, www.TheRestoreMovement.com, Facebook, and Instagram.

## Chapter Five

### Shushed into Shame
#### Tamra Andress

He pressed his pointer finger innocently against my lips in a shushed replication of his idolized heroes, the Three Stooges, as he revealed himself to me. I was scared and resistant, but naturally curious, as he forced my hand to explore the emotions further. My new backyard swing-set oasis emerged into a tainted secret hideout.

I was three, maybe four. Vivid first memories I suppressed so deeply out of confusion and shame that I could never comprehend the root of the problem—a problem that left me shackled for decades.

Exploration of sex and femininity long before my young heart could fathom purpose or my feeble mind could grasp guilt. Instead of seeking help, I sought the adrenaline, letting curiosity propel my secret actions. A couple years later during another innocent game, I discovered pornography magazines. That swing set became my regular spot, and I would hide in order to seek.

I sat disgraced behind the same bush as Eve in the garden; distraught over my decisions, equally confused over the flooded emotions. The major difference that left me entangled by the vines of the bush was blanketed indignity. We can comprehend and easily blame the deceptive evil serpent in the garden, but how do you cast fault on a culprit who was merely ten years old and mentally disabled?

I took the burden. I wore the responsibility. As if I was supposed to know better. Shouldn't I have known better? Shouldn't I have stopped it?

After the apple was eaten from the Tree of Life and the discovery of good versus evil was unveiled, Adam and Eve lost their innocent eyes. As years passed, I remained disgraced behind the bushes, even after God gave me clothes of dignity. I never felt like I deserved the fresh garments offered, because I kept eating the forbidden fruit all the while portraying to the outside world that I was dressed in white.

What started as innocent curiosity stemmed into deceptive teenage choices, consistently adding weight to the already heavy cloak of disgrace. The bizarre part was that I had no conscious understanding that I was struggling between two identities. I kept discovering people just like me. I didn't know I was broken. I didn't know I was lost. I felt, in opposition, like I belonged. I was just another typical teenager who didn't tell her parents all of the details, right? And so they kept inviting me deeper into what I thought and was being shown in every area of life as "normal."

Chat rooms, magazines, songs, commercials, photos, MTV videos—pop culture developed my self-image. Wasn't this what I was made to be—a woman, made for a man? Designed to please and cater to and comfort. My body, after all, wasn't meant for me. It was meant for my husband. And since I surely wasn't getting married yet, wasn't this only a natural path of exploration?

Even as I came to know Christianity in high school through a youth group called Young Life, I still felt justified. I read the books about waiting until marriage. I practiced it as long as I could, until the serpents showed themselves in multitudes, and I watched as others ate apple after apple. They weren't hurt. They seemed happier, even more feminine as their bodies blossomed. I succumbed to the desire.

Before highlight reels were a thing, I had managed to create a picturesque version of what I wanted others to see, while ignoring

> As years passed, I remained disgraced behind the bushes, even after God gave me clothes of dignity. I never felt like I deserved the fresh garments offered.

anything subsurface and masking all pro-
miscuities with other points of perfection.
I had flipped the script from the backyard
swing set—I was now the one asking
them to be quiet about our "play time";
I couldn't risk my parents or teachers or
"Christian" friends knowing what I was
doing.

He calls us His, which
determines our identity
first and above all. He
washes us white, which
frees us from our
secret sins.

And then the secret was finally out. I was immediately dismissed from my
youth-leader roles, kicked out of the organization, left alone, and disgraced by my best
friends. And yet, unlike Eve who had Adam to share in the experience, the "Adam" in
my garden was commended for his fruit-grabbing abilities while I was cast aside as a
harlot.

This was my opportunity. Stranded behind the bush, naked and afraid. Again,
God graced me with new clothes. But standing in the light, even clothed in something fresh, I felt dirty and vulnerable. *I didn't run to the people who could call out
WHO I was, and the people who could declare WHOSE I was had fled.* The only people
who claimed to "see" me and accept me were the same people who knew my weaknesses. So I sat behind the bush eating the apples alongside them, still trying to live
out the dual life of what was acceptable in the garden.

Years later, while standing in the light, God gifted me the man of my dreams,
the Adam who would see me and love me for the beauty I was meant to always
own. He reclaimed the innocence of the little girl on the playground. We explored
our faith together. We adventured together. We married and established our home.
And then we had children of our own.

And yet the serpent's trickeries still whispered from the outlying trees; I ignored them as often as I could. I didn't want to go back in the shade of hiding. The
sun on my face felt heavenly.

In hindsight, I should have cut down the tree. I should have taken the time to
comprehend how it got planted in the first place. We should have moved gardens.
But I had suppressed everything so deep, beyond recognition or remembrance, in
the desire to stay in the green my husband knew me for.

He clothes us with dignity and strength, which reclaims our innocence.

Just like God gave Eve the entire garden of Eden, we are given the entire garden to frolic in. Yet we stay stranded beneath the one tree that sucks life from our very body. We make choices out of emotion rather than wisdom. We develop habits that keep rotten trees fruitful. We let serpents determine our worth and shame determine our identity.

But there is good news. Our Father loves us so much that He created gardens more fruitful and luscious than what our heart or bellies could ever comprehend. And by His power and through His strength, we can chop down the serpent's trees, grind and uproot the destructive source, and replant goodness in the new fertile abundant soil that He helps us till with His mighty hands and grace-giving heart.

He calls us His, which determines our identity first and above all. He washes us white, which frees us from our secret sins. He clothes us with dignity and strength, which reclaims our innocence.

How freeing it was to finally uproot the tree and every single root that made it stand.

Uprooting is painful, but so is growing and birthing something new. And it doesn't happen by the power of your own hand. You need help from the very people whom God placed in your life to support you the whole way through, and ultimately your Ezer (helper), your Love, your Gardner.

This process is worth every effort of freedom that comes on the other side. Each root removal brought clarity and peace to years of pain and shame. And like the spring season, one day your newly planted good seeds will bear the fruit of the Spirit instead of the fruit of the serpent. You will take refuge under the ultimate Tree of Life. And you will stand boldly, proudly, and beautifully in the light of the sun. And I will rejoice alongside you.

## Resilient Truth

But the fruit of the Spirit is love, joy, peace, forbearance, kindness, goodness, faithfulness, gentleness and self-control. Against such things there is no law. (Galatians 5: 22–23 NIV)

## Resilient Prayer

*Lord*, I am wilted and I am lost. I feel shackled by my past, and I can't seem to come out of hiding, because I am ashamed of what I've done and what has happened to me. I am confused why this has transpired in my life, but I know You have greater purpose than my mind can comprehend and that my brokenness will be restored to the beauty You intended for me to exude.

God, I thank You that Your power is made perfect in my weakness. I thank You that You love me and are with me always. I thank You that Your name alone causes darkness to flee and that Your victory dismisses the isolating serpents that try to strand me in fear. I thank You that by Your strength and protection I am covered. That even before my mother's womb, You knew me and You purposed me for goodness and truth within Your kingdom. I am grateful that I am robed in the white of Your righteousness, no matter my past mistakes. And I pray that I lean on Your strengths, truths, and grace as I uproot the dead things in my life once and for all.

I know this won't be easy. But I trust in You alone. In Jesus's name. Amen.

I am robed in the white of Your righteousness, no matter my past mistakes.

 *Resilient Action*

What fruits are you currently eating that belong to the serpent?

What do you need to uproot from your garden in order to release the shame, guilt, or indignity that burdens you?

Read Galatians 5:13–26—the life-giving opportunity of bearing good fruit.

_____

_____

_____

_____

_____

_____

_____

_____

_____

_____

_____

Tamra Andress is an entrepreneurial passionista, ordained minister, retreat coordinator, and podcaster with Fit in Faith. She is a kingdom connector, seizing and sharing health, wholeness, and happiness by illuminating purpose and light within others! You can find her at www.fitinfaith.com, @fit__in__faith on Instagram, and Tamra Leigh Andress on Facebook.

Chapter Six

## My Father's Daughter
### Tanya Glanzman

We first met when I was six, shame and me. My parents went out for the night, trusting the television to babysit. A neighbor came by to drop off some keys. He stayed longer than he should and taught me games not meant for little girls.

As an abuse survivor, alcoholic, and drug addict, my mother knew shame well. Through poor choices that affected both of us, shame was invited into our lives to take up permanent residence. Her shame-based identity prevented her from loving me well. From the age of two to fourteen, seven different men stole from me things that were never meant for them to access. The first was my father, and the last was my grandfather. Each sacred intrusion wedged my soul open a little further, giving more room for shame to settle in and get comfortable.

One of the men claimed to have a close connection to God. We spent almost a year living with him in a small motel room beside a busy street. I spent my days locked in the bathroom, behind a door on a cold tile floor. This man, who claimed to be an angel, confirmed what I already suspected to be true. I was a bad little girl. There was a special place in heaven for bad little girls, he told me. I rocked back and forth to self-soothe as shame held me close, assuring me that I'd never be loved by anyone, including God.

My mother abandoned me when I was ten—moved away and had another little girl.

*Worthless . . . disposable . . . replaceable . . . you are so unlovable that your own mother doesn't want you.*

Believing the lies shame whispered in my ear, I began to repeat its mantra within. It echoed those who had failed to love me well. I began to live out my shame anthem by behaving in ways that proved it true.

There were many difficult years ahead. Shame was a faithful leader toward unhealthy coping skills. Suicide attempts, cutting, an eating disorder, addiction, promiscuity. Nothing quieted the screaming within my soul. Shame fueled each choice, assuring me this was what I deserved and all I was worth. There was something inherently flawed with me, and it was my fault. All of it.

When I accepted Jesus as my Lord and Savior at the age of sixteen, He graciously moved in. He and shame remained roommates for a long time, fighting over space in my heart, mind, and soul.

Jesus and shame accompanied me to church. On new, holy ground I tried to capture the love my heart longed for from those who also knew my Jesus. Unfortunately, having not been taught the rules of church or relationships, my passion outweighed my wisdom, and I presented as foolish and socially unacceptable. I was unlovely and hard to love, even among those who were called to be known by their love one for another.

Cloaked in insecurity, shame was a faithful thief of peace, reminding me if anyone ever knew who I *really* was, they too would realize I was not worthy of love. It was safer to stay hidden behind religion and achievement.

At twenty-one, my daughter was born. She was innocent and vulnerable, and I held her close. It was the mama in me who rose up to stare shame in the eye and to draw a line in the sand. I desperately wanted her to have a different life. I wanted her to know what it meant to be fully seen, fully known, and fully loved.

I traded in the efforts of striving for people to love me for the intentional seeking of God's love for me.

This was the catalyst for change in my

life. I learned I could not give what I did not have.

I traded in the efforts of striving for people to love me for the intentional seeking of God's love for me. Through learning truths found in His Word, I began to hear and value my heavenly Father's voice over all others. I exchanged my identity as a daughter who was abused and abandoned by her parents to a daughter of the King, who was fully known, seen, and loved.

The more we know who we are in Christ, the more our lives reflect the truth of who we really are and were created to be.

The Samaritan woman in John 4 knew shame too. Each failed relationship with men validated her unworthiness to be loved. Fear of judgment led her to the well during the hottest part of the day, when she would most likely be alone. But then she wasn't. Jesus was there, and in a very short conversation filled with hope and truth, He made her aware that she was fully known, fully forgiven, and fully loved. Jesus's living water washed away her shame and restored her joy.

In Luke 7:36–50 we meet a woman whose shame was known. Overwhelmed by gratefulness for the unconditional love Christ offered, she poured out her tears and perfume of oil to wash His feet. The shame dealers in the room judged her, which led to a teachable moment for all present.

*Those who have been forgiven much, love much.*

A shame-based identity leads to shame-based actions. The more we know who we are in Christ, the more our lives reflect the truth of who we *really* are and were created to be. Until this truth is realized, we often make choices that reflect who we are made to believe we are.

Proverbs 4:23 tells us to "keep our heart with all diligence, for from it spring the issues of life."

When we are young, we automatically trust those in authority to feed us truth. We keep what they say, hide it in our heart, and allow it to form our foundation. Before we have the ability to discern between a lie and truth, lies sneak in and plant themselves deep within our soul. Until those lies are identified and replaced with truth, we live out of them. This impacts every facet of our lives.

The only way to replace lies with truth is to know truth. John 8:32 (NLT) states,

> Choosing to shed the cloak of shame to embrace the robes of righteousness provided by your heavenly Father will enable you to live the life of peace and joy He created you to live.

"And you will know the truth, and the truth will set you free." In order to be free, we must *know* the truth.

Investing time and energy into learning God's Word is key in understanding the depth of His love for you. The more you learn the truths found in God's Word, the more you will understand not only who He is as a good, kind, and loving Father, but who He says you are as His loved and cherished daughter!

It was in the time spent with Jesus that I, the Samaritan woman, and the woman who was forgiven much were released from shame. It too will be where you are released from shame. Choosing to shed the cloak of shame that has been administered by the enemy of your soul to embrace the robes of righteousness provided by your heavenly Father will enable you to live the life of peace and joy He created you to live.

A transformation will begin to occur that will help you to see yourself through His eyes—understanding that His opinion about you is the only one that really matters.

Accepted rather than rejected.

Chosen rather than forsaken.

Called rather than forgotten.

Healed rather than broken.

Understanding that you are completely loved right where you are on your journey toward looking more like Him, you will be able to cease from striving. The hole in your heart will be filled by the One intended to fill it.

Then you will know the truth, and the truth will set you free. (John 8:32)

*Abba Father*, thank You for your unconditional, never-failing love. Help me to recognize and evict any lies that remain in my heart that do not align with what You say about who I am in and through Christ, my Savior.

Help me, Father, to see myself through Your eyes. To walk in the identity You have given me as a daughter of the King, rather than out of a shame-based identity.

Thank You, Father, that those who love much have been forgiven much. I am thankful for Your grace, mercy, and forgiveness. My heart is grateful for Your living water that washes away my shame and never leaves me thirsty.

I praise You, Father, for being my source of love and affirmation above all others. Help me never to allow any voice to rise above Your voice of truth in my life and in my heart.

> Help me, Father, to see myself through Your eyes. To walk in the identity You have given me as a daughter of the King, rather than out of a shame-based identity.

*Resilient Action*

Examine your heart and ask God to help you recognize any shame-based lies that are impacting the way you interact with others and live your life.

Search God's Word and find truths to replace those lies. Meditate on those God truths until they become truer than the lies.

Accept God's forgiveness for any behaviors born out of a shame-based identity and begin to embrace being fully known and loved.

Tanya Glanzman, LPC, writes and speaks as My Father's Daughter. Offering hope and encouragement wrapped in grace-filled truth, her heart is that every woman would know what it truly means to be a daughter of the King. Connect with her at www.myfathersdaughter.com, Facebook, and Instagram.

# Part 2

# Loss

## Chapter Seven

# The Day the World Changed
### Tammy Trent

As we walked into the room, two attendants were wheeling a table through another set of doors. On the table was a body covered with a sheet. *Trent's body.* We watched as they pushed the gurney into the center of the room. Then one of them pulled back the sheet, and there was Trent.

He lay there in that familiar dive suit, and he looked so perfect, as though he were sleeping. Unstoppable tears flowed down my cheeks and dropped onto his face as I leaned down to him and whispered desperately, "Can you just wake up, Trent? Can you just wake up? You're right there. You're lying there. Can you just wake up?"

He looked beautiful, perfect. Apparently no creatures had touched him. There wasn't a single scratch on his face. I touched his leg, and it felt soft and surprisingly warm. I kissed his face once, and then again. It too felt soft and surprisingly warm. He looked so handsome, so perfect. Even his hair was just right, spiked up a bit in just the right place and lying smooth against his head everywhere else. Then I noticed a little line of blood coming from his ear—it had dripped onto the paper covering the table. That bothered me, seeing the blood on Trent. I felt my legs tremble, and black splotches filled my vision.

Dad, feeling me sway, tightened his grip on my arm and held me up.

In a moment I nodded that I was okay, and he released my arm and stepped around to the other side of Trent, squatting down so he could look more closely at his head, trying to see where the mysterious injury had occurred. He wanted to get a better look at what had happened to his son.

We had been told that Trent had not died because of drowning but because something had hit the back of his head. Later we would see the autopsy report that blamed death on "multiple contusions to the head." Whatever hit him—maybe a boat, maybe a piece of coral—had knocked him out and prevented him from surfacing for air.

Dad straightened up and said, "Okay, let's go."

I bent again to kiss Trent's forehead, then we walked out. We had been there less than ten minutes. It was the last time I would ever see my beautiful Trent.

I wish now that I could have stayed longer. I wish I could have had some time alone with Trent to talk with him, pray beside him, sing to him.

So much had happened in such a short time. Just two nights before, I had fallen asleep beside Trent in a world that seemed steady and secure. Now, forty-eight hours later, I felt as if I had lost everything. Trent was dead, and the whole world had erupted in chaos. I had only caught bits and pieces of the news throughout the day. Lost in my own grief, I could barely imagine that the same grief I was feeling was being shared that night by the families of nearly three thousand others on September 11, when terrorists attacked the United States, the same day my Trent died.

The images were so painful that I didn't watch much TV as the days passed in my hotel room in Jamaica. But late one night when I couldn't sleep, I turned it on and was thankful to find a Christian station. And even better, there were my friends in the Christian musical group Selah. They were singing a song I recognized immediately, and at that moment I felt as if they were singing it solely to me. The song was "Press On," and I sat there singing along with them, "In Jesus's name, press on."

We couldn't have gone home even

So much had happened in such a short time. Just two nights before, I had fallen asleep beside Trent in a world that seemed steady and secure. Now, forty-eight hours later, I felt as if I had lost everything.

if we had wanted to go then, because no one was flying into the US yet. But I was adamant that I wasn't leaving Jamaica without Trent. Meanwhile, paperwork and other requirements had to be completed before the Jamaican government would release the body to be shipped back to America. Trent's Dad handled everything, for which I was grateful.

For me, the long days of waiting in the Jamaican hotel continued, and each seemed longer than the day before. My Trent was gone. I wanted my mom. And she couldn't get to me. We kept thinking that I would be coming home soon. *Surely the airlines will start flying again soon, and how long can this paperwork take?* After Trent's Dad went back home, I lay on the bathroom floor and wailed. I sobbed and moaned and cried so loudly the hard-tiled walls of the bathroom seemed to echo every sound.

In the midst of my brokenhearted tirade, I had this tearful conversation with God: "If all this is real, if You are real, if heaven is real," I sobbed, "could You just send somebody to hold me? God, could You just send somebody? I'm not asking for a hundred angels. I'm just asking for one special angel, just one angel who could hold me right now. God, You're so big . . . if You can hear me, if You care . . . please do this for me."

Then I heard within me the words *Get up and move.* Surprised and a little shaky, I rose to my feet. It took every ounce of strength I possessed to move toward the door, open it, and step out into the room. The tears flowed again, and I held on to the doorframe and peered out from the bathroom and through the adjoining doorway. A short, slightly chubby Jamaican woman wearing a Hilton housekeeping uniform was standing there in Dad's room.

I wiped my face and said to her, "Excuse me, ma'am, but could you just come in and make my bed? I've got my sheets all wadded up in the bathroom, and I've made a mess of everything."

When she saw me, her beautiful, smooth black face reshaped itself into a sym-

In the midst of my
brokenhearted tirade,
I had this tearful
conversation with God:
"If all this is real, if
You are real, if heaven
is real," I sobbed, "could
You just send somebody
to hold me?"

> *That morning I had asked Him for an angel . . . and here she was. As she held me, I felt the arms of Jesus embracing me, comforting me, supporting me.*

pathetic expression of concern. "Oh! I've been trying to get to you," she exclaimed with her sweet Jamaican accent. "I could hear you crying, and I've been trying to get to you."

Then she paused and took a step toward me. "Could I just come and hold you?"

The moment she stepped toward me, I started to cry again, nodding my head, biting my lip, tears coursing down my cheeks. She had heard me as I'd lain on the floor of that bathroom and cried out to God.

Who knew angels wore Hilton housekeeping outfits? She was an instant answer to prayer, a godsend. She wrapped her arms around me, and I dropped my head on to her shoulder and sobbed. I felt so comforted in that moment, so reassured that God is real. All my life I had taken Jesus for granted, just always assumed He was there, an invisible but ever-present force in my life. That morning I had asked Him for an angel . . . and here she was. As she held me, I felt the arms of Jesus embracing me, comforting me, supporting me. With my head against her shoulder, she started whispering into my ear. At first I couldn't understand, but then it became clear. *Of course! She's praying for me, exactly what an angel would do.*

Then she held me back to look into my face. "You're grieving, aren't you?" she asked with concern covering her face. "You've lost someone, haven't you?"

"Yes," I whispered. "My husband."

"Oh no! But you're so young!" She prayed again, eyes closed, earnest words winging themselves upward.

Later as she worked to tidy up the room, she sang. It took me a moment to realize what I was hearing. She was totally off key, but the words were clear. She was singing praises to the Lord, and it was the most beautiful sound I'd ever heard. It was as if my tone-deaf Trent were singing to me, and to Jesus, through this gentle angel in the housekeeping outfit.

I smiled, listening to her as I sat at the desk in Dad's room. The Gideon Bible lay there, and I reached for it. *Speak to me through Your Word, God. Please, don't make me hunt for it. I'm too wrung out now to think clearly. Just let me open up this Bible and find a message to me from You. Please, Lord, don't make me climb a mountain, walk through a valley, and struggle through the jungle to figure out what You want me to know right now. I just ask You to meet me here and show me.*

I opened that Bible, and immediately my eye fell on a specific verse: Psalm 30:5. This is how I read that passage:

> Although, you may mourn throughout the night and sorrow will endure throughout the night—probably throughout many nights, Tammy—My joy will always come in the morning. My joy will always meet you in the morning. When you feel like you can't breathe, when you feel like you can't walk, when you can't see, when you can't get through the day, I'm still there, carrying you. When you can't breathe one more time, then just rest your head on the pillow, and I'll be right there beside you. When you wake up the next morning, I'll be right there beside you. My joy will cover you. And joy will be the very thing that will bring you back to life again, because without it, you'll never survive this grief. Just trust Me, Tammy. Trust Me.

Amazed, even shocked by how vividly Jesus was reaching out to me, I rose from the desk and walked to the huge window looking over the city and the water. I stood there, staring *out* that window, and incredibly I felt joy, unspeakable joy, heavenly joy. There was nothing in my life that made me happy at that moment, yet I felt unspeakable joy.

When I first lost my husband, it seemed impossible to even breathe. Shock, then sadness, and sometimes fear, literally took my breath away. But God's healing came into my life one day, one step, and even one breath at a time. Today I am not only breathing again, I am dancing. Connie Neal

When you feel like you can't breathe, when you feel like you can't walk, when you can't see, when you can't get through the day, I'm still there, carrying you.

God's healing came into my life one day, one step, and even one breath at a time. Today I am not only breathing again, I am dancing.

wrote a book called *Dancing in the Arms of God* to describe how it felt to follow the Lord through life's difficulties. At first I could not imagine ever dancing again. Ever being that happy. It was a struggle just to sit up and get out of bed. But I could feel the very presence of God reaching out to me. I could sense the prayers of my family and friends when I couldn't pray myself. There was hope in that for me.

This story is not just my life's story. All who risk loving, risk losing the one they love. Sometimes that loss comes through death of the one we love; other times love itself seems to have died when a relationship is broken. In every loss, we have to look to the very source of love, to Jesus Christ, for strength to keep pressing on. He has given us precious promises in His Word to bring the pieces of our lives back together. The Bible is like an eternal love letter that will give us hope through all of life's trials and unite our hearts with His.

When you draw near to God in times of trouble, you learn who He really is. Then you learn that

> You can trust Him.
> He is not sitting in heaven on a throne
>     but walking with you here on earth.
> He wants a personal relationship with you.
> You can know the depth of His love for you.
> Your soul craves relationship with God.
> You can call on Him for help first,
>     not after other sources have failed.

The Lord is close to the brokenhearted, and he saves those whose spirits have been crushed. (Psalm 34:18 NCV)

## ~ Resilient Prayer

*I don't understand* anything right now, Jesus, but I know You didn't do this to me. You love me more than that. You would never take _____ from me. I don't get it. I don't see how this could be good for my life. How could living without _____ be good for me? He was the only _____ who never left me. Now he's gone, and I don't understand. All I know is, I trust You. You've been with me before. I've always been a fighter, always survived whatever came my way. So I guess I just have to fight through this thing too. I hate that I have to do that. But You've been with me before, and You'll be with me through this too.

In every loss, we have to look to the very source of love, to Jesus Christ, for strength to keep pressing on. He has given us precious promises in His Word to bring the pieces of our lives back together.

 *Resilient Action*

Name your loss and pray your boldest prayer to God, telling him exactly what you need. In fact, write it here in this book. Watch and believe that God wants to answer your heart cry.

---

Tammy Trent is a recording artist, author, and speaker. But on September 11, 2001, her songs ceased while she spent time healing after the tragic death of her husband while on a missions trip. A year later she returned as a speaker and performer at women's conferences. A gifted communicator, she draws her audience close with her energetic personality, and yet the sincerity of her heart is woven through the very words she speaks.

## Chapter Eight

# That Time I Crawled under My Desk
## Brenda-Lee Sasaki

I knew for quite a while that things were not right—things within me, things at the church I had ministered in and worked at my entire life. As I child and young adult I was nurtured in this steadfast, faith community with women and men who became my aunties and uncles, my Sunday school teachers, girls' club mentors, choir directors, lifelong friends. They planted seeds of grace and wonder, cultivated my curiosity and love for Jesus, and empowered my growing hunger to study Scripture and theology at deeper and deeper levels.

And it was very good for a long time.

Until it wasn't.

And then it was very bad.

People move on. New staff members are called in and called away. Times change; fashions certainly do. And cultures shift. And rightfully so. As we mature in our lives, our careers, our experiences, our faith, these new pieces of information reshape us in meaningful and profound ways.

What I was not prepared for, however, was that me and my church would soon take such divergent paths during these seismic shifts.

When I began to question inherited ideologies that no longer made sense and did not seem to align with these new theological discoveries I was making, rather than engaging in this uncomfortable dance together, I increasingly found myself being dismissed, misunderstood, and alone.

I went from being respected, influential, and safely ensconced in the center of the vocational work I was clearly called into, that I had loved and given the very best I had to offer, to finding myself one afternoon huddled under my desk, weeping uncontrollably and experiencing such paralyzing anxiety that crawling under my desk seemed the safest place I could go to protect myself.

The church broke me.

More specifically, a flawed leadership structure that was not willing to be held accountable for accommodating destructive, controlling, and abusive behavior.

And I left my job and the only church community I had ever known . . . forty years of my life. And now it was all taken away by people who should have had my back, the people I thought were looking out for me.

*Where were you, God? Why didn't you defend me? You could have stopped this from happening.*

So I get why Hagar ran away.

She was an immigrant woman in a land that was not her own. She was a slave to an angry barren woman, who likely herself was suffering shame and guilt because of her infertility, both privately and publicly, in a culture that deemed a woman's sole worth by the number of children she bore. And she was sexually exploited by a man who refused to take responsibility for the role he had to play in these events.

> Now Sarai, Abram's wife, bore him no children. She had an Egyptian slave-girl whose name was Hagar, and Sarai said to Abram, "You see that the Lord has prevented me from bearing children; go in to my slave-girl; it may be that I shall obtain children by her." And Abram listened to the voice of Sarai.
>
> So, after Abram had lived ten years in the land of Canaan, Sarai, Abram's wife, took Hagar the Egyptian, her slave-girl, and gave her to her husband Abram as a wife. He went in to Hagar,

and she conceived; and when she saw that she had conceived, she looked with contempt on her mistress.

Then Sarai said to Abram, "May the wrong done to me be on you! I gave my slave-girl to your embrace, and when she saw that she had conceived, she looked on me with contempt. May the Lord judge between you and me!" But Abram said to Sarai, "Your slave-girl is in your power; do to her as you please." Then Sarai dealt harshly with her, and she ran away from her.

The angel of the Lord found her by a spring of water in the wilderness, the spring on the way to Shur. And he said, "Hagar, slave-girl of Sarai, where have you come from and where are you going?" She said, "I am running away from my mistress Sarai." The angel of the Lord said to her, "Return to your mistress, and submit to her." The angel of the Lord also said to her, "I will so greatly multiply your offspring that they cannot be counted for multitude." (Genesis 16: 1–10 NRSV)

Hagar was at the mercy of her masters. She did what was required of her. She was exploited by women and men who wielded exacting power over her, and then when things got complicated, she was tossed aside.

*Dismissed, misunderstood, alone.*

I knew those feelings intimately.

Did you notice that they did not even speak Hagar's name? She was referred to as *slave-girl* by both Sarai and Abram. You see it's easy to strip away someone's humanity when their identity is reduced to their status, their powerlessness, or their failures.

*Troublemaker. Sinful woman. Spirit of Jezebel.*

These were some of the names assigned to me. It's easy to make someone a target of our anger and therefore treat them in ungodly ways when we characterize them to suit the narrative that justifies such behaviors.

The angel of the Lord called her by her name, Hagar, thereby restoring her dignity, her humanity, her personhood.

Her encounter with God
made her faith possible
and her trust in their
new relationship tangible.

And in her running away to protect herself and her unborn child, she was found. Truly found. And the angel of the Lord called her by her name, Hagar, thereby restoring her dignity, her humanity, her personhood. Because the God of Abram and Sarai was also the God who saw all that was, all that was immediately present, and all that was to come.

So when the angel asks her where she was going, she didn't know. Of course she didn't know. All she knew was that she just had to leave.

So he tells her to go back. And while it may seem puzzling that the angel would send her back to an unsafe situation, consider this: She is not going back as a nameless, powerless slave-girl. She is returning as Hagar, the mother of Ishmael, who will be a great yet troublesome man (kids are complicated!). Moreover, Hagar is given the exact same covenantal promise that was given to Abram (Genesis 12:7). Nowhere else in the biblical texts do we see a profound levelling of the playing field.

For Hagar, going back was a defiant act of resiliency.

Her encounter with God made her faith possible and her trust in their new relationship tangible. Unlike Sarai and Abram, who took matters into their own hands when God spoke to them about His abundantly gracious plans for their futures, Hagar took step after dusty step right back to the place and the people that tried to break her.

And I love the final response Hagar utters out loud. For she, in redemptive mutuality, names God in the most profound, relationally connective way: "So she named the Lord who spoke to her, 'You are El-roi'; for she said, 'Have I really seen God and remained alive after seeing him?'" (Genesis 16:13 NRSV).

After a year of therapy, a lot of rest, and time to reimagine what the next steps for me would be, the God who sees invited me back into kingdom work, albeit on an entirely new playing field and in a new position where I got to call the shots.

I spent the next six years in graduate school working on two degrees, eventually leading me to coaching certification, new pastoral roles for a time and season, and into the academic world of teaching servant-infused leadership theory and practices to up-and-coming global leaders.

Church today looks a lot like deep conversations about leading with integrity and wholeness, with twenty-two-year-olds standing in front of fluorescent-lit classrooms with whiteboards and PowerPoints, marking papers, challenging perceptions, changing ways of thinking. And I show up every day thanking God that he found me, alone and anxious on the August afternoon, entering that hopeless space under that desk alongside me and loved me enough not to leave me there.

## ⟿ Resilient Truth

But as for me, my prayer is to you, O Lord. At an acceptable time, O God, in the abundance of your steadfast love, answer me. With your faithful help rescue me from sinking in the mire; let me be delivered from my enemies and from the deep waters. Do not let the flood sweep over me or the deep swallow me up, or the Pit close its mouth over me. (Psalm 69:13–15 NRSV)

## ⟿ Resilient Prayer

*Oh God*, everyone has let me down. Those whom I thought could be counted on are nowhere to be seen. I feel hopelessly alone. I don't know where I am even going, but I know I don't want to go back to where I was.

God, I know that You see me. I believe that You are with me even now, even when I don't feel You close by. So I will remember Hagar that in her desperation, You found her. You called her by name. You restored her. You took care of her. You blessed her. God, I would boldly ask you for the same. Please find me. Please call me so I can hear You. Please restore my heart, soul, my body, my faith. Please take care of me. Please bless me. In Jesus's name. Amen.

*Resilient Action*

Acknowledge that people have let you down. Name them. Beside their name, record exactly how they have let you down. *Be specific.* Then invite God into each of these situations, asking, "Lord, what do You see when You look at each of these people and each of these events? Can You show me what You see so that I can also see with Your eyes? What is true? What is at the core of each of these painful situations? As the God who sees my past, my present, and my future, what do I need to do with each of these disappointments in order to move forward?"

_____

_____

_____

_____

_____

_____

_____

_____

_____

_____

Brenda-Lee Sasaki grew up on the West Coast of British Columbia, Canada. Recovering from perfectionism, growing up Baptist, and finding her voice has fueled her resolve to bring her full, curious self to the places and spaces she finds herself, whether teaching, speaking, writing, or igniting others to go and do likewise. Connect with her at brendaleesasaki.com or Facebook and Instagram.

Chapter Nine

## The Club We Do Not Choose
### Celeste N. Bowers

For all those who have lost hope and purpose—for all those who hurt deep inside from loss—I wish I could protect you from all pain and suffering. I could not shield my own ten-year-old daughter, Christina, from the storms. I was not allowed to trade places with her. God specifically chose Christina for a magnificent job. She had to be His representative. Christina accepted this position with her bright smile and sweet spirit. Although I still can't protect anyone from life's tragedies, I can tell you this—and I am proof of this—no matter how hard you fall or how much you ache, God will lift you up. He will carry you out of the weeping waves and safely to shore. He will restore your strength and renew your purpose.

## The Club We Do Not Choose

I did not sign you up, Christina, nor did I enlist our family for this type of membership. As parents, we strive to involve our children in the best organizations and activities that are a perfect fit for the skills our children possess. We spend hours filling out applications that include the simplest questions, such as our children's names and birthdates. Yet that can all change in a moment. In a second we may be faced with involuntary circumstances we cannot fathom. Suddenly we find ourselves in a club we did not choose.

In life, though, we can choose how we react. We can attempt to cancel any membership or escape any situation we haven't chosen and turn away from God, or we can accept the situation and represent Christ through the ordeal.

Oh, Christina, how could we ever choose anger and emptiness over Christ? Jesus suffered. Jesus wept. Jesus lives. You hurt. You cried out—and you live through Him.

Were you watching over my shoulder every time I filled out school applications for Teddy? Did you ask God to move me and guide me as I decided I would never leave blank spaces? Inevitable questions took my breath away. For example, most questionnaires asked for the number of children in a household. I always wrote "two" because I will always have two children. Then the applications asked for the names and ages of those children. It punched me in the gut every time, but I never wavered from my answer—writing your name and the age you entered heaven.

Even though I still put your name on applications, your name, Christina Natalie Bowers, is written in a much more permanent and special place—the Book of Life. What your name symbolizes remains constant as well, as I was reminded by a story about a dream our friend Jane had about you.

The night before Thanksgiving in 2010, Jane dreamed about you. In this dream, you were a teenager—the age you would have been that year. You appeared healthy, and your thick hair had grown back. You stood above Jane—perhaps signifying the heavens above. You smiled and said, "Christ is in me." Jane asked you to repeat what you said, and you repeated, "*Christ* is in me. He's always been in me. He is the first six letters of my name!"

No matter how hard you fall or how much you ache, God will lift you up. He will carry you out of the weeping waves and safely to shore. He will restore your strength and renew your purpose.

Jane woke up counting the first letters of your name and knew this truth: you are in heaven, and Christ lives in you. He lived in you every day here on earth, and now He lives in you in eternity.

How could we ever choose anger and emptiness over Christ? Jesus suffered. Jesus wept. Jesus lives. You hurt. You cried out— and you live through Him.

What makes the timing of Jane's dream even more special is that the day before Thanksgiving is the day we had been told about your cancer years earlier. It is such a sad memory, yet the pain was washed away by the meaning behind that beautiful dream. Once again God knew what I needed and what our family and friends needed at that time.

My name, Celeste Natalie Bowers, has not changed over the years, yet my role has been altered. I am still your mom, but I am also your voice now. My lifetime status in this club that we did not choose has been achieved. Through this membership, I wish to personify your best qualities and serve Christ fully. You are the light in my heart, and Jesus is the light of the world.

Do you remember that promise we made when you were faced with the cancer diagnosis? The commitment we made to each other in that hospital room stands the test of time and applies to me now just as it did years ago. Even in the saddest moments, I never ask, "Why me?" Instead I pick up my sword and combat any dark emotion with the words, "Use me. Use me, Lord, for Your name and Your glory!"

As a part of this club, I desire to keep my eyes and heart open to help other members. Our journeys are all different, and we walk through these traumatic storms in our own way. Nevertheless, there is one common thread. There is one constant tie: God. He is the Master Weaver of this stunning tapestry called life. This exquisite creation holds patterns that go beyond edges, yet He connects us all in His perfect timing. Christina, I proudly carry this precious thread to help connect people until I enter heaven. I cling tightly to every unique piece—each remarkable person—knowing that through God's promise of heaven, I, too, will feel whole again.

Finally, my brethren, be strong in the Lord and in the power of His might. Put on the whole armor of God, that you may be able to stand against the wiles of the devil. For we do not wrestle against flesh and blood, but against principalities, against powers, against the rulers of the darkness of this age, against spiritual *hosts* of wickedness in the heavenly *places*. Therefore, take up the whole armor of God, that you may be able to withstand in the evil day, and having done all, to stand. (Ephesians 6:10–17 NKJV)

*Resilient Prayer*

*Dear Lord*, people still ask me, "How do you do it? How do you watch your daughter walk through such a storm and then go on after she has passed away?" My answer is quite simple. "How could I watch my own daughter carry her cross with such a sweet, gentle spirit for Christ and not pick up and carry mine?" As I pick up my own cross and carry it through these years, my prayer is to grasp every moment and make them all count. Christina recognized at such a young age that her journey was not about her. The impact of her words, "It's not about me. It's about Christ working through me," live on today. It is not about me either, Lord. Even though Christina is gone, time continues to march forward. I don't view anything here on earth in the same way now. When Christina entered

Even in the saddest moments, I never ask, "Why me?" Instead I pick up my sword and combat any dark emotion with the words, "Use me. Use me, Lord, for Your name and Your glory!"

heaven at the age of ten, my life seemed to me to be out of order, but it did not seem so to you, Father! It was according to Your plan. What helps me move gently through time is nothing by my own means. Instead, I trust You, Lord,

How could I watch my own daughter carry her cross with such a sweet, gentle spirit for Christ and not pick up and carry mine?

wholeheartedly to navigate my path and offer me purpose. Your ways become my ways. "For my thoughts are not your thoughts, neither are your ways my ways, saith the Lord. For as the heavens are higher than the earth, so are my ways higher than your ways, and my thoughts than your thoughts" (Isaiah 55:8–9 KJV).

## Resilient Action

When someone we love passes away, especially a child, nothing seems to fit. Nothing is in order. But to our Lord, things are in perfect order. He is the thread of all that fits. How will you lean on Him, trusting that He still has an amazing plan and purpose for you? Are you willing to be used mightily as you share the hope of Christ and promise of heaven with others and help them heal spiritually? What clubs or groups will you choose that can strengthen you inside and out? We must seek opportunity to rebuild that which sadness has broken within us. We may not fully understand any of this until we get to heaven, because we are not of this world. "And do not be conformed to this world, but be transformed by the renewing of your mind, that you may prove what *is* that good and acceptable and perfect will of God" (Romans 12:2 NKJV).

How will you lean
on Him, trusting
that He still has an
amazing plan and
purpose for you?

Christina's life and testimony live on through her mom, Celeste Bowers, in *If There's a Mailbox in Heaven* and *When Your Voice Became Mine*. She shares about her newfound purpose through her writing and motivational speaking. Follow Celeste N. Bowers on Instagram, Facebook, and at www. mailboxinheaven.com.

## Chapter Ten

# The Loss of a Dream
### Patti Fagan

**Overwhelmed with grief and heartache,** I sat on my bed and sobbed uncontrollably. We had been meeting with our pastor for marriage counseling for the past several months. But that morning I met with my pastor alone. We were no longer meeting with Pastor as a couple. We were divorcing.

As I stared out the window, feeling a deep sense of hopelessness, I cried out, "Why, Lord?" In frustration I then screamed out, "Why can't you save my marriage?" I felt utterly defeated and let down by God.

I had always dreamed of having a family, a home of our own, and living happily ever after. When I realized the dissolution of our marriage was inevitable, I prayed even more earnestly that God would not allow us to be another divorce statistic. I prayed, "Please, God, don't let us end up in divorce. Please don't let my marriage dream die."

After we separated, I couldn't help but feel that God let me down. Why wasn't He answering my prayers? The sadness and loss of my marriage dream made my heart sick. My marriage was one of several losses that occurred over a short period of time. Earlier that year, we'd lost our business. Then after we separated, we lost our home to foreclosure.

It felt like my entire life was being ripped away, that God was taking from me everything that mattered. I wrestled with emotions, doubting God, and the loss of my identity. Who was I now that I wasn't married? Where did I go from here? Why was God allowing all of this to be taken from me?

A dear friend of mine, who was always there to impart sage advice, assured me everything happens for a reason, and that God had a better plan for me. But that's not what I wanted to hear at the time. I didn't want to trust God with my life if it meant I had to suffer this agonizing pain.

Many years had gone by before I came to realize that I was not disillusioned by God but by the Enemy, who had me believing I knew better than my creator about what was best for my life. When I finally came to see that my heavenly Father had my back the entire time I was going through the divorce, I repented for doubting His love for me. I chose to trust His plan and surrendered to His will for my life. I allowed myself to relax into the comfort and assurance of His loving arms. I was like the prodigal son running back to his father's house after a season of foolish living.

Sometimes we think we know better than God, especially when it comes to major life circumstances. We tend to always perceive loss as a bad thing. While grieving the loss of someone or something we love is tremendously difficult, the pain so excruciating we'd rather die, it's not until we look back in retrospection that we are able to see the mighty hand of God at work on our behalf.

Throughout the Scriptures, God promises that He has good things planned for our lives. That all things work together for good (Romans 8:28). He promises to give us a future and a hope (Jeremiah 29:11). Yet we doubt His love for us when things don't go the way we think they should.

As it turned out, the losses I experienced were actually a blessing in disguise. Just as my wise friend assured me, God did have a better plan for my life. One that I couldn't possibly have imagined because I was feeling so sorry for myself.

Little did I know then that one day I would marry again. But

> I came to realize that I was not disillusioned by God but by the Enemy, who had me believing I knew better than my creator about what was best for my life.

this time to a man who treats me like a queen, that we would have a beautiful home together, and that I'd be sitting here telling you my story from a place of peace, restoration, and happiness.

Today, as I look back on that season of loss, I can't help but identify with the biblical story of Naomi and the devastation she felt when she lost her husband and two sons. Her story is found in the book of Ruth:

Little did I know then that one day... I'd be sitting here telling you my story from a place of peace, restoration, and happiness.

> But Elimelech, the husband of Naomi, died, and she was left with her two sons. These took Moabite wives; the name of the one was Orpah and the name of the other Ruth. They lived there about ten years, and both Mahlon and Chilion died, so that the woman was left without her two sons and her husband.
>
> Then she arose with her daughters-in-law to return from the country of Moab, for she had heard in the fields of Moab that the Lord had visited his people and given them food. So, she set out from the place where she was with her two daughters-in-law, and they went on the way to return to the land of Judah. But Naomi said to her two daughters-in-law, "Go, return each of you to her mother's house. May the Lord deal kindly with you, as you have dealt with the dead and with me. The Lord grant that you may find rest, each of you in the house of her husband!" Then she kissed them, and they lifted up their voices and wept. And they said to her, "No, we will return with you to your people." But Naomi said, "Turn back, my daughters; why will you go with me? Have I yet sons in my womb that they may become your husbands? Turn back, my daughters; go your way, for I am too old to have a husband. If I should say I have hope, even if I should have a husband this night and should bear sons, would you therefore wait till they were grown? Would you therefore refrain

from marrying? No, my daughters, for it is exceedingly bitter to me for your sake that the hand of the Lord has gone out against me." (Ruth 1:3–13 ESV)

The loss of Naomi's husband and two sons was more than she could bear. Her heart was shattered, her pain unendurable to the point of bitterness. So much so that she even tried to change her name from *Naomi*, which means "pleasant," to *Mara*, which means "bitter."

But she said to them, "Do not call me Naomi; call me Mara, for the Almighty has dealt very bitterly with me. I went out full, and the Lord has brought me home again empty. Why do you call me Naomi, since the Lord has testified against me, and the Almighty has afflicted me?" (Ruth 1:20–21 NKJV).

In her anguish and heartache, Naomi didn't know that God had a beautiful plan of restoration and blessing in store for her. She lost her sons, but God gave her a daughter, Ruth. Ruth married Boaz, and they provided for Naomi, which was a substantial blessing for a widow.

God also used Boaz and Ruth to bless Naomi with a grandson, Obed, who would eventually become the grandfather of King David. Now, instead of calling her Mara (bitter), the women of the city called Naomi *blessed*. Even though Naomi, in her grief, could not feel the lovingkindness of God, it did not stop Him from touching her life in spite of her bitter circumstances. He turned her story of heartbreak and loss into a story of redemption and blessing for her and for others.

The bottom line is this: God wants us to know that He loves us and we can trust Him. Yes, even when we are devastated, feeling the grief of an unbearable loss of someone or something we love. When we are brokenhearted, we can know that He is close to us (Psalm 34:18). He wants to be the Father who comforts us in all of our troubles (2 Corinthians 1:3–4).

> Even though Naomi, in her grief, could not feel the lovingkindness of God, it did not stop Him from touching her life in spite of her bitter circumstances.

He knows our destinies before we're even born (Psalm 139:16) and He knows how things will turn out in the end. He gives us a hope and a future. If only we would allow ourselves to be comforted in His presence, we would come to trust that He has everything under His control, that in the

*Revive and refresh me that I may feel Your healing love and peace saturate my soul.*

end He makes all things work together for good. Just like He did for Naomi. Just like He did for me. I know He'll do it for you.

## Resilient Truth

For I know the plans I have for you, declares the Lord, plans for peace and not for evil, to give you a future and a hope. (Jeremiah 29:11 NKJV)

He heals the brokenhearted and binds up their wounds. (Psalm 147:3 NKJV)

## Resilient Prayer

*Father*, show me how to trust in your love for me. Help me to see how You have my back even when I don't understand why I'm experiencing this loss. Help me to continue in Your Word, seeking comfort and refuge in Your loving arms. Revive and refresh me that I may feel Your healing love and peace saturate my soul. Let me not focus on the pain and sorrow that grips my heart, and instead cause me to be uplifted by Your all-consuming love. Cause me to see and feel Your presence in unexpected ways as I go about my day, knowing You are always with me and You never leave me. I choose to trust that this season will pass, that though weeping may endure for a night, joy comes in the morning (Psalm 30:5).

## Resilient Action

In what way can you choose to surrender your grief to God and trust that He has a future plan for you?

What changes can you make in your daily routine that will support you through your season of loss?

How can you make the decision to move on with life in spite of your circumstances? (Just like Naomi did when she became instrumental in arranging Ruth's marriage to Boaz.)

Patti Fagan is an award-winning life coach, Ramsey Solutions Master Financial Coach, and bestselling co-author of *Supercharge Your Success*. You can find her online at www.pattifagan.com, www.pattifagancoaching.com, Facebook, LinkedIn, and Instagram.

## Chapter Eleven

## *Lost Is Findable*
### Kim Cusimano

Words can be tricky. Recently I have been thinking of two in particular, "lost" and "loss." These words sound similar, but one has turned my world upside down more than the other. I have a favorite of the two and one I can't shake. I prefer and favor "lost."

As a mom, like all moms, I wear an invisible superhero cape that can help find just about any item lost around our house. A lost shoe? No problem: I reach under the dirty laundry pile on my son's floor and rescue the moment, finding the shoe no child would have found in infinite years of looking. Lost schoolbook? Too easy: under the seat of the minivan! How about the ketchup bottle my husband could not find in the fridge? Please, give me a real challenge! Wearing my invisible cape, I take a calculated risk and bet my hubby that his lost ketchup bottle is behind the butter. Score . . . I win!

But "loss"? Whereas lost things can be found, loss feels strangely permanent. Loss feels like continually trying to find something I already know is gone forever. I have been living in a getting-acquainted phase with loss, and it's proven to be a worthy opponent.

The loss of a beautiful mind—if only it was just lost, I know as her mom

> Loss feels like continually trying to find something I already know is gone forever.

I could find it. Our daughter was four when we noticed she liked talking to the walls more than she talked to us, her family. She was seven when we heard the words "childhood-onset schizophrenia." Now, at age twenty-one, she sits in my living room with eyes aimed at faraway places or at people only she can see. The weight of loss fills the room. In childhood, doctors and medicines helped us to keep much of her mind with us. She had a cute, gentle personality and ability to express herself clearly. As a family, we lived and thrived, at times even prideful in celebrating how tightly and determinedly we had held on to her. Adolescence proved to be a sneaky thief. The years began to steel from us parts of our daughter's mind we thought we had successfully preserved. We live here now, in a new place of loss. A loss that is so often hard to put into words or at best uncomfortable to talk about with others.

As I have been getting acquainted more intimately with loss, I've learned there are still treasures that can be found. I can't control the loss—there is a permanency there that has ushered me into moments of panic and grief. But some things have been lost to me in the middle of loss, and I realize I can still find these things if I choose to look. I can find peace in exchange for panic, comfort in the midst of grief, compassion in the difficult, and joy in hard days.

What about you? Do you need to join me in finding these things? Have you lost your peace or joy in the middle of your loss? We are in good company! The disciples could relate. There was a particular day they lost their peace and had picked up absolute panic. Listen in on Luke 8:22-24 (NASB):

> Now on one of those days Jesus and His disciples got into a boat, and He said to them, "Let us go over to the other side of the lake." So, they launched out. But as they were sailing along, He fell asleep; and a fierce gale of wind descended on the lake, and they began to be swamped and to be in danger. They came to Jesus and woke Him up, saying, "Master, Master, we are perishing!"

Perishing! Now, that's panic! And, you know what? That's where I've been on some of these recent days, weeks, months, and years of loss. As mental illness has stolen from us, I keep losing my peace and picking up panic. More and more frequently our daughter is talking to her own imagined world, and when we try to break through to her, we often get an agitated response, as if we don't belong in her world. She yells, sometimes curses, and on her really bad days, screams at the top of her lungs. This has become our wind-tossed boat, our fierce storm.

Honestly, some days if I rely only on my feelings, I would say it feels like Jesus is sleeping during my storm too.

After He calmed the storm, there is an amazing question Jesus asked the disciples in verse 25: "Where is your faith?" Doesn't it sound like they had just temporarily lost something? The thing is, they had lost it, but Jesus knew at the asking they could find it again.

Some things get lost—on some days it's our faith, other days our peace, maybe our joy too, or all of the above. In Jesus, these things can be found, and beautifully, again and again. The disciples inherently knew they had to find Jesus first. Remember back to verse 24: "They came to Jesus and woke Him up . . ." If we are going to find what we need in the middle of loss, in the middle of our own brewing storms, we first need to find Jesus. In Him can be found the saving calm.

Sometimes I make the first step of finding Jesus too complicated. Religious jargon can easily parade across my mind or my own made-up religious formulas for approaching Him. The disciples simply called out, "Master." Secondly, they told Him they were about to drown. You and I can do this. We can call out "Master" and tell Him we fear we are drowning. That's the ultimate finding, finding the One who controls the wind.

I've learned there are still treasures that can be found... I can find peace in exchange for panic, comfort in the midst of grief, compassion in the difficult, and joy in hard days.

Many years before the disciples found themselves in the storm, the prophet Isaiah was trying to teach the children of Israel the same principles. God used Isaiah to record His words: "My lovingkindness will

Some things get lost—on some days it's our faith, other days our peace, maybe our joy too. In Jesus, these things can be found, and beautifully, again and again.

not be removed from you, and My covenant of peace will not be shaken" (Isaiah 54:10 NASB).

"My lovingkindness will not be removed from you"—it sounds like even if Israel felt they had lost that "lovin' feeling," it was there for the finding. God was not removing or hiding His lovingkindness. What God provides, stays! We have a tendency to lose sight of God's provision, especially in loss. In loss, our gaze is often fixed on what we cannot regain or find. We have to refocus our eyes on Jesus first, and then we will be able to see all that is found in Him.

## Resilient Truth

"For the mountains may be removed and hills may shake, but My lovingkindness will not be removed from you, and My covenant of peace will not be shaken," says the Lord who has compassion on you. (Isaiah 54:10 NASB)

## Resilient Prayer

*Lord*, thank You that You are findable! You are in my storm, in my loss. Lord, I choose to find You first, then to set my eyes on all Your provisions of peace, comfort, security, compassion, lovingkindness, faith, joy, and hope. Lord, help me not to fix my gaze on loss but on these things that can be found in You.

Lord, help me to see others who are dealing with loss and to be a compassionate guide and encourager, leading them to You when they can't see You for themselves.

## Resilient Action

How would you describe your loss? How do you need Jesus to help you? Are there things in Jesus that you have lost but that can be found, such as His peace, His comfort, His compassion—how can you go about asking His help to find these things?

In loss, our gaze is often fixed on what we cannot regain or find. We have to refocus our eyes on Jesus first, and then we will be able to see all that is found in Him.

Lord, thank You that You are
findable! You are in my storm,
in my loss. Lord, I choose to
find You first.

Kim Cusimano is founder of Full Joy Ministries. She is an author whose
poetry and articles have been published in several compilation books. As a
mother to two special-needs adults, she spends her time encouraging those
around her to reach their full potential. Contact her at kim@cusimano.us
or FullJoyMinistries.com.

## Chapter Twelve

# When You Can't Feel Your Legs
### Karen Neeb

Everyone knows the possibility that *the* call might come. Like the angel of darkness, we hope, perhaps even pray, that it will pass us over, that it will go to someone less deserving. It is never a call you expect to get. It knocks you out of everyday life and into a tailspin of surreal nightmarish pieces of a life you do not recognize.

This call came Sunday, July 14, at 1:00 a.m. I knew something was wrong. There were doctors from a hospital three states away and a social worker on a speakerphone. Nothing personal about this call. No bedside manner. No *Greys Anatomy* hug.

This is how I found out my oldest daughter, Allison, my mini me, was killed as a passenger in a single-car accident, her fiancé at the wheel. Their words sank deeply in my ears, tore out my heart: "Your daughter is deceased. There was nothing we could do." They asked, "Do you have any questions?" I realize some might want details; my only thought was, *Wow, my daughter is dead. What else could I possibly need to know?* As all feeling left my body (yes, you do go numb), no questions, probably for the first time in my life, came to my mind. Other than *What do I do now?*

Six months before, my divorce had been finalized. I felt lost and found myself wandering a local Christian bookstore looking for something, anything, to avoid this feeling. I found Stormie Omartian's book *Just Enough Light for the Step that I Am On: Trusting God in the Tough Times.* I was drawn to it, as I quoted this often as the way we take steps of faith, one at a time, and God gives us enough light to see our feet. We need faith to take a step.

Reading Stormie's book engulfed my life, transformed me. Little did I know then that God was preparing me for that devastating phone call on July 14. I developed deep personal growth during this time. I thought I had an idea of what God wanted, where God was moving me, but oh, how He surprises us.

I am thankful for that time. I call it my "time-out period," as I was looking for a part-time job, and every door was closed. Even a simple food-service job that a high schooler could get, I was told no. It was apparent to me that God wanted me to sit still and spend time with Him. I learned to lean into Him, listen to Him, and trust Him. This time of dependence and obedience was my refuge when I lost Allison.

One of the first people I called that night was my girlfriend. We talked on and off all night. Something she said me got me through not only the first few days but still helps today: "The Bible says our days on earth are numbered." I looked up the whole verse to make sure it was not Hallmark erroneously quoted; it was not. "Your eyes saw my unformed substance; in your book were written every one of them, the days that were formed for me, when as yet there were none of them" (Psalm 139:16 ESV). This simple statement allowed me to not hold the driver of the car, my daughter's fiancé, responsible for the accident. In my mind, according to Psalm 139:16, July 13, 2019, was Allison's day to be called home no matter what she was doing or where she was.

What quickly became apparent was

It was apparent to me that God wanted me to lean into Him, listen to Him, and trust Him. learned to lean into Him, listen to Him, and trust Him. This time of dependence and obedience was my refuge when I lost Allison.

the army of faithful, godly women the Lord had strategically been placing in my life over the previous couple of years. I have always been an introvert, keeping real friendships at a distance. However, much to my chagrin, more women were entering and staying in my life. I was making friends, going out, sharing life. I had Bible study women— referred to as FROG (fully rely on God) ladies. When my life took this drastic, unexpected left turn, these women were from a Meetup group of five hundred women—most I did not know—and they wrapped themselves around me like a blanket of love. I realize now how important it is to put yourself out there and make real connections. These people show up in the bad times. The first calls and cards I received were from women I did not know but knew of me from groups we shared.

The Bible says our days on earth are numbered. This simple statement allowed me to not hold the driver of the car, my daughter's fiance, responsible for the accident.

These acts of godly love continued to let me know God was with me. He had not abandoned me. He had been taking time, preparing me, surrounding me with His angels on earth to take care of me and give me the visible strength added to the invisible strength I felt from Him every time I cried out to Him. Ecclesiastes 4:9–10 (ESV): "Two are better than one, because they have good reward for their toil. For if they fall, one will lift up his fellow. But woe to him who is alone when he falls and has not another to lift him up!"

Now, as I lay on the floor, sobbing, I did the only thing I knew to do. I cried out to God. I asked Him, begged Him to take away the crushing pain in my chest. I knew He was the only One who could truly be the guiding force through this darkness. I asked Him to hold me. I leaned into Him and gave Him my load. It was too much for me to carry. And throughout the grieving process, I was always in God's arms, protected and loved. Eventually the crushing pain in my chest lifted, and God took my pain. Yes, that sounds nice, and you are thinking that I may have been in shock. Do not get me wrong—I cried and I still cry. I have panic attacks at grocery stores or large gatherings. The difference is now they are manageable and I pray without ceasing. I know God will not abandon me.

There are several versions of the cliché God does not give you more than you can handle. I can tell you, firsthand, He does. This is a sentimental statement delivered to those going through tough or grieving times, to make the other person feel better. I think they believe we are strong enough to get through it, but how many people do not? How is it explained away? The truth is, God gives us what we can handle when we lean into Him. "My grace is sufficient for you, for my power is made perfect in weakness" (2 Corinthians 12:9 esv).

As my ex-husband and I made the trip together on Sunday morning to Nashville from Michigan to take care of the details, we arrived at the apartment and parked next to Allison's car. We opened the back of her car and found cases of water she'd bought to hand out to the homeless. My daughter had had a huge heart for the homeless from the time she was old enough to realize they were homeless.

One of the first things I found in her car on the dashboard was her Bible. I opened it, and it was marked up, written in, and had notes in the concordance. Now, I like to use her Bible each day, and I love opening it and finding her notes and the things she thought were important. Not only does God speak to me through her Bible but my daughter's notes as well. I also knew she loved her church—she talked about it and the people often.

As I move forward into my new life without Allison, I am aware and more heightened with compassion when I hear of a mother losing a child.

I believe I have two choices on how this loss will define me. It will crush me, and I will stop living, become a shell of who I am and perhaps wait and hope to die. Or I am not just living my life but that of my daughter, whose life was cut short at age twenty-six. A happy, loving, giving, laughing young woman. She devoted her time to working in the nursery at church and making homemade cookies for the homeless, because she knew they probably never got something homemade.

I choose to honor her by doing things she

> There are several
> versions of the
> cliche God does not
> give you more than
> you can handle...
> The truth is, God
> gives us what we
> can handle when
> we lean into Him.

can no longer do. I believe God will give me the strength and He will continue to direct my steps as I give Him the glory.

You alone are the
answer to the healing
I so desperately seek.
When my brokenness
is too much for words,
let me know You are
with me.

## Resilient Truth

Trust in the Lord with all your heart and lean not on your own understanding. In all your ways acknowledge Him, and He shall direct your paths. (Proverbs 3:5–6 NASB)

## Resilient Prayer

*Lord God, my loving Father and Comforter*, in times of loss and sorrow, You are the constant we can lean into and hand our brokenness. Thank You for a love so great. You alone are the answer to the healing I so desperately seek. When my brokenness is too much for words, let me know You are with me. You know my needs, and You will not abandon me. Give me hope for a future when I cannot see past the pain of today. Surround me with love and encouragement so that my days will be less lonely. Remind me of the happiness, when my mind drifts to sorrow. For You are the God of love and joy. Let me see that this dark road has an end, with You walking with me every stop of the way. In Jesus's name. Amen.

Give me hope for a future
when I cannot see past the
pain of today. Let me see
that this dark road has an
end, with You walking with
me every stop of the way.

 *Resilient Action*

How is your relationship with God? Is it strong enough to handle
a great loss? Or even a small loss? Do you believe He will truly
carry you through a tough time? Write some ideas of ways to a
deeper relationship with God.

_____

_____

_____

_____

_____

_____

_____

Karen Neeb is a blogger and aspiring author. Writing is her outlet, and you
can find her creating at livinglifethroughlyrics.com and ponderasigo.word-
press.com. Much of her time is spent volunteering with local and national
organizations. You can connect with Karen on Facebook and Instagram.

# Part 3

# Abortion

## Chapter Thirteen

### The Truth that Sets You Free
#### Annette's Story, by Lorraine Marie Varela

From the start of her life, Annette felt her voice did not matter. The pain of molestation, and her molester's threats that she couldn't tell a soul, overshadowed the joy of carefree childhood days. Inner turmoil led her to the conclusion that she was unlovable, a person without worth. Because she didn't believe she could be loved for who she was, she detached from feeling love for herself or for others. Instead, Annette sought to earn love through performance. The truth of her identity was crushed.

As Annette grew older, the need to achieve significance continued to be a driving force in her life. If she could impress others, she would prove she was a lovable person, so she set her sights on becoming an architect. At nineteen years old, Annette was pursuing her dream and in a stable, happy relationship with her boyfriend—a relationship that could one day lead to marriage. Her boyfriend was thoughtful and kind, and he often brought roses to express his affection for her. When Annette learned she was pregnant, the future she envisioned was forever altered. She couldn't fathom how she'd be able to love her baby when she couldn't even love herself. Her emotions toward the baby were completely numb. Embarrassed and ashamed, she wanted to hide. She had been raised in a good Christian

> For the first time, I felt deep, deep sorrow for the loss of a person.

home but had turned away from her faith. If her parents found out about her pregnancy, it would demonstrate she was unworthy and unlovable, so she kept her secret hidden from them. She felt she had nowhere to turn. No one stood by her side to encourage her or tell her, "You can do this. I believe in you!"

Friends steered her to an abortion clinic, where the doctor and the nurses offered their counsel. "You should abort. That's the best decision for you." Naïve, scared, and vulnerable, Annette trusted their advice, as they seemed to know what they were talking about. But the clinic was unable to perform her abortion. An ultrasound revealed Annette was sixteen weeks pregnant, much farther along than she'd thought. "Your tissue is larger than allowed in Indiana," the technician told her bluntly. Annette felt the stinging chill of coldness emanate from this worker. It took her by surprise, and she wondered if the technician's job had contributed to the deadness of spirit that hardened her soul.

To have an abortion, Annette would have to cross state lines to Kentucky, where the abortion laws were more lenient. The following day, Annette's boyfriend drove her to Kentucky to an abortion clinic. He also felt pressure to live up to high moral standards set by his parents, but had fallen short. Out of desperation to hide his failure from them, he became complicit in the decision to end his baby's life.

Before she had her abortion, Annette didn't know what she was stepping into. However, the *moment* her abortion was complete, she had a spiritual awakening. "I knew I had taken the life of an innocent person," she recalled. When she experienced the drastic sting of death, her emotions roared to life, awakening her senses to feelings that had been buried. "For the first time I felt deep, deep sorrow for the loss of a person," Annette said. The weight of guilt and shame washed over her. She could no longer look at babies or listen to their cries. These sights and sounds haunted her, and she ended the relationship with her boyfriend.

Giving in to abortion scarred Annette in more ways than she realized. She was terrified of becoming a mother. She was afraid she would hate her future children and abuse them. Because of her abortion, she felt she had partnered with the supreme child abuser, the devil. "Abortion is the worst form of child abuse there is,"

Annette said. "Because I partnered with him, I opened myself up to his voice in that area of abuse." The voice said she would be a bad mother—the voice that came from the Father of Lies.

Within a few years, Annette found herself pregnant again. This time she was married to a good man she loved, and it should have been the happiest time in her life—but she wasn't looking forward to bringing their child into the world. All her fears came flooding back. Yet the day she gave birth to their son, a miracle took place in Annette's heart. It was love at first sight. A new spiritual awakening overwhelmed her spirit—the revelation that she had bought into a dirty lie. She didn't hate her son. He didn't repulse her. The love she had for her newborn baby affected her profoundly. "This was the most amazing and joyful experience of my life," Annette said. In an instant, her mind understood a truth her spirit had known all along: *Abortion is wrong.* It wasn't just a piece of tissue that had been removed from her body. It was a baby.

Now the years following her abortion made sense. When she'd been feeling sad about her loss, her friends had deemed her baby insignificant and unlovable, invalidating Annette's feelings. They had told her, "You just had an abortion. There's nothing wrong with that." So she'd stuffed down her emotions, pretending the abortion hadn't bothered her. But in her spirit, she knew she had done something *really* wrong. She knew she had taken a life. With the permission to grieve denied, she'd had no place or space to mourn this loss of life. She'd *needed* to mourn her first baby's loss. It was the most natural thing to do. "And I couldn't," Annette said.

Grief over an abortion is rarely spoken aloud. Many who have aborted their children feel pressure to hide their emotions of grief and act like everything is okay. They don't realize that grief affects their entire being, whether they acknowledge their grief or hold it in. It is impossible to grieve and heal when you're worried about what other people think. Suppressing emotions is unhealthy, and to enter into healing and wholeness, you must be allowed to grieve.

Grief has a purpose. You wouldn't grieve if you didn't love.

After her son's birth, Annette continued to carry the heaviness of guilt and shame, unaware

Grief has a purpose.
You wouldn't grieve
if you didn't love.

that the same antilife spirit behind abortion affected every area of her life. "One abuse leads to another," she said. Child abuse, self-abuse, and thoughts of suicide afflict many women who have experienced an abortion. Annette was distressed when she discovered that her own mothering instincts were compromised. Whispered lies continued to assault her mind—lies that said she would be a horrible mother, unable to love her son or feel connected to him. The temptation to agree with these lies was ever present, and she fought to preserve the truth.

Annette returned to the roots of her faith and started walking closely with the Lord. Then the pieces of her past fell into place, as she understood a spirit against humanity had attacked her identity from her youngest days, but those thoughts had not originated in her heart. The spirit was a liar. As she learned how to distinguish her own internal voice from the voice of her enemy, she would positively affirm the truth. "I am a good mother," she'd say. "I'm a *loving* mother. I love my child. I love him more than myself." With each affirmation, her mothering instincts were strengthened as the lies fell away. She continued to fight against this spirit by standing fast on the truth of God's Word and wrapping herself in His love. During one of her times of worship and contemplation, Jesus gave her permission to mourn the loss of her first child. He promised to wipe her tears away. "That is when I received spiritual and soul healing," she said. "When I had permission to mourn, I sought Jesus for forgiveness. Then I had to forgive myself."

Annette shares wise counsel to anyone who is tormented by the trauma of abortion and needs to walk through mourning and forgiveness. She says, "Acknowledge there was a life, a purpose, and a destiny for your child. One of the most wonderful things you can do is give your child a name. Once you have named your child, acknowledge that God designed your child and that they were a person. God will then take you on a journey of forgiveness, love, and compassion you can't study for or know how to do on your own." Annette followed this advice herself. She asked the Lord to reveal to her the sex of her baby and named her daughter Rose to honor her child's birth father, even though he was no longer a part of

> When I had permission to mourn, I sought Jesus for forgiveness. Then I had to forgive myself.

her life. With her voice strengthened by love, Annette chose to bring value to Rose's life as she shared her testimony publicly, speaking out about her past and giving hope to others for their future.

Life is precious. Your life has meaning. It's not because of what you do, but because of who you are. You were created highly valuable and highly loved.

The road of grief has provided Annette with insights she might never have known otherwise. "When your identity is suffering—and you don't love yourself—it's easy to throw another person's life away," she said. She is now acutely aware of the need each person has for understanding and valuing their own purpose in life, and offers these words of hope. "Life is precious. Your life has meaning," she says. "It's not because of what you do, but because of who you are. You were created highly valuable and highly loved." This is the truth of *your* identity—the truth that will set you free.

## Resilient Truth

Lord, you know all my desires and deepest longings. My tears are liquid words, and you can read them all. My heart beats wildly, my strength is sapped, and the light of my eyes is going out. (Psalm 38:9–11 TPT)

## Resilient Prayer

**(God's Response to Your Prayer for Healing)**

My child, I will surround you with My love. My compassion reaches out and reaches in to touch those places left vulnerable and exposed. I will heal every wound of your soul.

It's easy to believe God loves others, but it might not be as easy to believe God truly loves you. You may believe in His love with your mind, even though you haven't experienced this truth in your heart.

Let your healing journey begin with this simple question: Jesus, why do You love me?

The Lord may give you a picture, or specific thoughts and impressions may come to mind. Record these thoughts now. Don't be afraid to receive. Open your heart and let His healing love flow.

Lorraine Marie Varela is the author of *Planned from the Start: A Healing Devotional*, written to invite readers to begin healing from the pain of post-abortion trauma to freedom and wholeness. She and her husband, Gabriel, co-founded *Inspiring Faith International*, a ministry to help people from all walks of life draw closer to God. Together they co-led a prayer and ministry team on the film set of *Unplanned*. Lorraine and Gabriel live in the Los Angeles area and can be found online at www.inspiringfaith.us.

Chapter Fourteen

## Fear Makes the Wolf Bigger than It Is
### Andrea Tomassi

"You're the one who asked for this," the nurse whispered in my ear after hearing me moan and cry during the procedure.

I was just fifteen years old.

I should have known better, so I thought. I became a Christian at the age of five while watching a Billy Graham Crusade on TV with my mother—I asked her where everyone was going. Reverend Graham had asked if there was anyone who wanted to receive Jesus Christ as their personal Savior. I remember seeing lines and lines of people in the aisles and wanted to know where they were going.

"Honey, they want to ask Jesus to come into their hearts," my mother replied.

"Well, I want to ask Jesus to come into my heart too," I cried.

She grabbed my hands and explained to me the meaning of the sinner's prayer, and I made my choice to accept Jesus into my heart.

Growing up, I can't remember a time when we didn't attend church. Most Sundays after church were followed by antique shopping, which my parents loved to do on the weekends. They both had stressful jobs. My father worked long hours for a restaurant chain, and my mother had the hardest job of them all, in my opinion—stay-at-home mom to me and my siblings.

Memories of sitting in the backseat of our gold Lincoln Continental with my sister and brother, holding on to lights, furniture, ceramic vases, and whatever else couldn't fit in the trunk while listening to the Imperial singers on an eight-track deck.

The following years were spent trying to balance being the good Christian girl at church and the popular cheerleader while dating my high school sweetheart.

I was so terrified to tell my parents that I was pregnant, but even more ashamed of what my grandparents would think of me. So that made the choice easy.

No one would ever know, and legally I didn't need my parents' permission. I believed if I went through with this pregnancy, I'd be the black sheep of the family, forever banned and labeled an outcast. "You will let everyone down if you have this baby," I kept telling myself.

Fixing everyone else's problems and taking on their emotions as my own was an everyday occurrence. I thought it was a good thing to want to "help" people! Maybe some of you reading this can relate to codependency and people pleasing. I have always struggled this way for as long as I can remember.

There is truth to the German proverb "Fear makes the wolf look bigger than he is!" But fear is not from God. "For God has not given us a spirit of fear, but of power and of love and of a sound mind" (2 Timothy 1:7 NKJV).

I come from a legacy of God-fearing people who have trusted God and depended on him for *everything*! But this? No way! There was no way I could live with them looking at me differently.

About five years ago, I started the process of dealing with the trauma from my abortion experiences, and God used the year I separated from my husband to draw me closer to Him and finally forgive myself.

But at fifteen, what I just couldn't wrap my head around was knowing there were other girls who didn't know Jesus, yet they'd made a different choice. Why couldn't I do that? Why did I sacrifice my morals for comfort?

The same situation arose two years later as I found myself pregnant again. The same thoughts flooded my mind, and I had my second abortion at the age of seventeen.

A storm was brewing on the horizon, and I never saw it coming. Satan would use the very thing I'd loved the most to break me. I'd been singing in church since I was eleven, and later had voice lessons twice a week, with dreams of spreading the love of Jesus through the gift of music. My plan was to travel with a Christian group and

A thief never steals from an empty vault. . . there was something mighty inside that little girl.

tour the country as soon as I finished high school. It was all I could think about.

Since we know a thief never steals from an empty vault, Satan knew there was something mighty inside that little girl, and he would stop at nothing to try and destroy her future. Each time I would take the stage on Sunday morning, I would hear inside my head, *Who do you think you are? Standing up here in front of all these people, acting like a good little Christian girl? You're a fake and a fraud! You will never be able to use your gift again after what you've done!*

I didn't understand my true identity is found in Jesus or that I was "God's special possession"—1 Peter 2:9 (NIV): "But you are a chosen people, a royal priesthood, a holy nation, God's special possession, that you may declare the praises of him who called you out of darkness into his wonderful light."

Instead, I believed the lies and stopped singing in church and attending all together.

My choices affect the way I view myself; they have compromised my identity and distorted my view of God and His perfect, unconditional love for me. They drastically impacted the way I parented my children—overprotective because I didn't see God as forgiving and compassionate but rather as a stern and punishing God. I was always fearful that something bad would happen to one of my children, or worse, and I was basically waiting for the other shoe to drop.

I truly believed that in time God would punish me by taking one of my kids because I had taken one of His. This mindset of guilt, condemnation, and shame manifested over time into living a life of perfection and false humility.

Words from my heart to my fingertips usually flow when I write, often without effort. But if I am to be honest with you, after all these years, this was a challenging chapter to write. Not because I am ashamed—I know I am a new creation in Christ Jesus—but because of the millions of women who suffer in silence like I did for thirty years, and it breaks my heart. It is my prayer that my story can make

*Guide me to fully open my heart so I can release the shame from my choices so I can be made whole again.*

an impact for you to find freedom and finally be released from the horrible lies you've believed for so long.

Maybe you have never told a soul what you've done. If this is true, do you know how much your Father in heaven loves you?

Can I tell you something?

Nothing can separate you from God's love! *Nothing*! (See Romans 8:38). There is nothing you can say or do that will make Him love you any more than He does right this very second. It's not earned, friend. It was given to you as a gift, on a hill called Calvary, free to whomever asks. Ephesians 2:8 (ESV) says, "For by grace you have been saved through faith. And this is not your own doing; it is the gift of God."

There is also the second half of my story I want to share with you, the redemption chapter.

First, I have rejoined the worship team at the same church I grew up in, and today when those lies filter in, I say these three words: "Not today, Satan!" Today, I stand and sing with **BOLD** confidence. "In the day when I cried out, You answered me, and made me bold with strength in my soul" (Psalm 138:3 NKJV).

Second, after my husband and I reconciled in 2014, both of our oldest children were expecting. Two baby boys were born in 2015 in the same month, only three weeks apart. What is the significance to this resilient-faith story? The first time I held both of my grandsons in my arms, I gazed into their beautiful eyes and heard Jesus whisper:

> *I know how much you wanted to become a Mimi, and I know you would have been just as thrilled with one beautiful healthy baby boy, but this is what I have done for you because I love you so much:*
> *I have done exceedingly and abundantly more than you imagined.* (Ephesians 3:20)
> *I will restore to you the years the swarming locust has eaten.* (Joel 2:25)

*I am working all things out for your good.* (Romans 8:28)
*I am working in you for my good pleasure.* (Philippians 2:13)
*Hold on to those beautiful babies, and have peace knowing that I am holding yours until you can hold them one day.*

I cannot put into words the overwhelming grace, peace, and love I felt in that moment. God sees your pain, sister, and He's been waiting for you to let go.

## Resilient Truth

And I am convinced that nothing can ever separate us from God's love. Neither death nor life, neither angels nor demons, neither our fears for today nor our worries about tomorrow—not even the powers of hell can separate us from God's love. (Romans 8:38 NLT)

## Resilient Prayer

*Father God,* Your love for me reaches the heavens. I know I am Your child, made in Your image. Help me to see myself the way You do, perfect and holy in Your eyes. Guide me to fully open my heart so I can release the shame from my choices so I can be made whole again. Protect my thoughts so that they align with who You say I am, a precious daughter of the King. Protect me from anything that wasn't sent by You, Father. Thank You in advance for what You are going to do in and through me.

Nothing can separate you from God's love! Nothing! There is nothing you can say or do that will make Him love you any more than He does right this very second.

 *Resilient Action*

Are you holding on to guilt and shame for decisions you've made in your past? Jesus died on the cross so we wouldn't have to carry the burden any longer. When we hold on to old hurts and allow them to define us, we are looking away from the cross. What do you need to let go of? What lie are you believing? Get quiet with God this week and ask Him to show you what you need to work on.

Andrea (Andi) Tomassi is the author of the award-winning *Live Bold: A Devotional Journal to Strengthen Your Soul* devotional. She founded Transcended Ministries, inspiring women to rise above their circumstances and claim their identity in Christ. She believes no hurt is ever wasted and longs to bring a message of hope as she shares resilient stories of bold faith.

Chapter Fifteen

## Disqualified
### Kathy Buckey

It was unexpected, which is what made it so difficult to escape. One minute we were laughing about who knows what, and the next minute the question was posed that would impact me for years to come.

The five of us women were on our way home from a Bible study leaders' conference. There had been solid teaching, worship, and even Spirit-filled silence during the weekend. I felt better equipped and more confident in my calling to lead women in Bible study than ever before. The conference had been so good! I was relaxed, my guard down, and I was totally unprepared for what was to come.

One woman asked the question almost as a challenge: "Who in her right mind would think that she could be a Bible study leader if she's ever had an abortion?" I'm sure there was further discussion on this topic by the others in the vehicle, but my mind had come to a dead stop, almost as though I had been thrown into Park while driving down the freeway. I'm surprised the other women in the car didn't hear the collision in my mind.

All my reason, will, and strength went to work keeping me from being exposed as a fraud, *disqualified*. In my mind, the wall that had been taken down slowly brick by brick immediately went back up, now ever fortified. Within a moment all I had gained at the conference was washed away and I was left undone, uncovered, and exposed.

I accepted this distortion, that my sin, although forgiven, had *disqualified* me for Christian leadership.

Now I know it wasn't my friend's intent to be hurtful or judgmental, but it felt like both. The Lord had brought me to the place where I'd found forgiveness for my abortions. He had shown me that His grace, His shed blood had been enough to cover all my sins. So where was this accusation and condemnation from? From a friend, someone I did ministry with, someone who knew the Bible as well as I did. Unlike me, she hadn't committed a *disqualifying* sin.

We hide things we are afraid will bring us shame and dishonor. It's difficult to say the word even now, and it should never be taken lightly. My secret was abortion. Your secret might involve a different sin. Regardless of the sin, secrets keep you in bondage.

I knew the Lord had set me free, but there something missing. Forgiveness doesn't end at redemption but with full restoration. I'm not the only one who missed this truth; my friend missed it too.

When God freely forgives, He remembers our sins no more and the guilt and shame are removed.

The difficulty comes when we experience judgment from others when we attempt to share our hidden past. We feel, and others may even tell us, the long-forgiven sins from our past *disqualify* us for service in the kingdom in the present.

This false belief came through loud and clear in the question that was asked on that late summer morning. Even if God does not have a hierarchy of sins, some people do.

The Enemy has a way of twisting God's Word, doesn't he? There is a history found all the way back in Genesis, when there were only two people and when a daily walk with God was literal. The Evil One is so predictable that he whispers the same question to us from Genesis: "Did He say . . ." He loves to bring doubt, and if we're not careful and attentive to God's Word, we can buy into that lie.

We hide things we are afraid will bring us shame and dishonor.

As humans that makes sense to us. Our civil and criminal laws judge more harshly and require more severe consequences depending on the weight of the offense. God's redemptive offer does not. We need to make sure we are following God's truth without unconsciously adding our own conditions.

I was under the impression I had to just do better. When we ask people to "just do better," we cripple them, set them up for despair. Just doing better is not part of God's redemptive plan. Let's look at what Scripture has to say about this.

In Psalm 107 (ESV) the psalmist says four times, "Then they cried to the Lord in their trouble, and He delivered them from their distress." Some of the situations were not in response to something they had done. Verses 4–9 talk about a people wandering aimlessly and not finding a city to dwell in. They were hungry and thirsty. The Lord's response was to deliver them, satisfying their hunger and thirst.

However, verses 10–16 introduce individuals who are sitting in darkness, prisoners in affliction and irons due to their rebellion, their choices:

> Some sat in darkness and in the shadow of death,
>   prisoners in affliction and in irons,
> for they had rebelled against the words of God,
>   and spurned the counsel of the Most High.
> So he bowed their hearts down with hard labor;
>   they fell down, with none to help.
> Then they cried to the Lord in their trouble,
>   and he delivered them from their distress.
> He brought them out of darkness and the shadow of death,
>   and burst their bonds apart.
> Let them thank the Lord for his steadfast love,
>   for his wondrous works to the children of man!
> For he shatters the doors of bronze
>   and cuts in two the bars of iron.

They too cried out to the Lord, and he delivered them. Verse 14 says, "He brought them out of darkness and the shadow of death and burst their bonds apart." Verse 16 continues, "For He shatters the doors of bronze and cuts in two the bars of iron." This is some powerful imagery. No slipping you in the back door, into a back pew, silent. All of that freedom work was loud! Don't you think that must have gotten people's attention?

It is verse 15 that is the call of the redeemed: "Let them thank the Lord for His steadfast love, for His wondrous works to the children of man." Those of us who were once prisoners of shame and fear must be willing to do what is called for in Psalm 107:2! "Let the redeemed of the Lord say so, whom He has redeemed from trouble!"

If we do not speak out, how many others will remain imprisoned by shame, not using their gifts even though they have been given the same status of any of Jesus's followers—redeemed and fully restored!

It is my heavenly Father I want to praise! It is His love, His pursuit, His pardon that sets me free—and when I say free, I mean FREE! Free to love, free to serve, free to shine a light for those still in hiding.

Each time I have shared my story from shame to restoration, I have been approached by at least one woman who hugs me and whispers in my ear, "This is my story too." There are many safe places for you to get help in this process. For me that was the PACE program at CareNet. I urge you to seek God's wisdom in finding the place that is right for you.

If, on the other hand, you see yourself as my Bible study friend, believing that God has various levels of forgiveness or redemption, I urge you to read through Psalms. God responds to His people when they cry out, and never do we see Him differentiating them by the sins He has forgiven.

Let us not be a stumbling block to someone coming to Jesus because we feel their sins are too heinous to be forgiven, and let us not keep any forgiven believer from serving in the kingdom to their highest calling or gifting.

So if the Son sets you free, you will be free indeed. (John 8:36 ESV)

## ~ Resilient Prayer

*Heavenly Father*, we come to You ever humbled and grateful for Your redemptive plan that allows us to come to You acknowledging our sin, asking for Your forgiveness, and receiving Your full restoration. Let us live our lives in response to Your truth, always willing to share the testimony of what You have done for us to those around us. In light of what You have done for us, may we never withhold the truth of full restoration by words that bring shame and keep those who are seeking truth from finding You. In Jesus's Name. Amen.

May we never withhold the truth of full restoration by words that bring shame and keep those who are seeking truth from finding You.

## Resilient Action

So where do you find yourself in this story?

Are you the one still in hiding? Do you feel *disqualified* for any reason, perhaps not just by abortion but any forgiven sin cloaked in shame?

Kathy Buckey lives in Santa Maria, California, with her husband, Mike. She has two grown daughters and three grandchildren. She has led women's Bible studies, mentored women, and loves emceeing women's retreats at Redwood Christian Park. She is passionate about sharing the redemptive power of God's Word.

Chapter Sixteen

## No Pain Wasted
### Athena Dean Holtz

I woke up groggy from the anesthesia, clutching my empty abdomen.

My baby . . . my baby was gone.

My soft center, the place where my heart should be, felt like a rock.

*I will not cry. I will not cry.*

The man who said he loved me was gone. He'd started walking away . . . easing out . . . when I told him about the baby.

*I guess he isn't going to leave his wife for me after all.*

*Used. I feel used, like a crumpled old tissue.*

"Your life will be ruined, Athena. The last thing you need is a baby."

*No. The last thing I need is to trust anyone.*

*I'll never let anyone use me again.*

Studying and school didn't rank high on my list of choice activities. I got in trouble for talking too much. My mind was on riding my horses and showing them on the weekends. Homework was not important to me, nor was trying to fit into the cool cliques. I didn't even go to my high school graduation; I was competing at a horse show instead.

My friends and I were beginning to experiment with LSD, mescaline, marijuana, and hash. We'd cruise bars, and I'd look for guys to flirt with, usually from the band, to make me feel special. The trauma of my molestation had sown seeds of sensuality and promiscuity that erupted in my late teens.

At nineteen and in my first year of college, I got pregnant by the lead guitar player in a well-known Chicago-area band. I was determined to keep the baby. The baby's father had told me again and again, "I'm going to marry you. I'm going to leave my wife and marry you."

*Maybe he will keep his promise if I have the baby.* But I knew he was already easing out of the relationship and the responsibility of a child.

Three months pregnant, I finally admitted my predicament to my parents. My dad was dead set against me having this baby. "No way, Athena," my dad lectured. "Your life would be ruined. The last thing you need is the responsibility of a baby. I will make the necessary arrangements. I'll take care of everything."

I had no idea what this decision would do to me emotionally, but I allowed my dad to take over and clean up my mess. I had an abortion at a hospital under general anesthesia, though this was still an illegal procedure in 1972.

The day afterward, I lay, heartbroken, in my little brother's bed in his room, nearly delirious with a raging fever from toxemia. My parents had moved into a small condo without a room for me. Somehow, that no-room-for-me thing was symbolic of my life then.

Deeply hurt, I felt taken advantage of and used. I didn't allow myself to feel the depths of the pain of the loss of my baby, the betrayal of the broken relationship, or the abortion. I hardened my heart. *I will protect myself.*

That's when I made the vow.

*I will never let anyone use me again.*


## Realizing My own PTSD

Fourteen years later I found myself a Jesus follower and in full-time ministry working with Vietnam veterans and their families. The conference at CBN was packed to the gills with veterans and their wives. As I stood before these men and women, I was beginning to see in myself, and many of the other women married to vets, those same symptoms of PTSD, but not because we were married to vets:

1. Flashbacks, nightmares, intrusive thoughts
2. Isolation of self and family
3. Emotional numbing and constriction
4. Depression
5. Anger and rage
6. Anxiety, nervousness
7. Guilt
8. Denial
9. Thoughts of suicide
10. Substance abuse

PTSD was not just for veterans . . . many of us had our own, and God was lovingly pointing it out so that we, too, could allow Him to come in and heal those ravaged places.

No, PTSD was not just for veterans . . . many of us had our own, and God was lovingly pointing it out so that we, too, could allow Him to come in and heal those ravaged places that had been shoved aside and stuffed away because they were too painful to confront.

## Post-Traumatic Stress Defined

> PTSD is a natural reaction to an unnatural situation. The individual has experienced an event that is outside the range of normal human experience. The distressing event is persistently relived, and the individual deliberately avoids anything that could remind them of the distressing event or becomes numb to general responsiveness. (Chuck Dean, *NAM VET: Making Peace with Your Past* [Multnomah Publishing, 1990].)

Let's face it. Traumas are hard to wrap our heads and hearts around. These extremely emotionally destructive situations are hard to make sense of, so a person will typically either go crazy from the pain or harden their hearts and stuff it away

> One thing I know about our heavenly Father—He never wastes our pain.

and move into denial. From one extreme to the other, that's a typical human response to something so horrific that we just can't make sense of it.

## Stuffing the Pain Only Makes It Worse

While this fact isn't necessarily part of the definition, it's what I've found to be true about PTSD. It most often seems to manifest in a life if the trauma and its associated feelings have been stuffed, and the survivor avoids dealing with them in an unconscious attempt to escape the pain.

That is exactly what I did with the pain of my abortion. How about you?

Certainly, as a Christian, we need to surrender these areas of suffering to the Lord and allow Him to have His way in healing us. Too often we seem to think because we're saved and have given our hearts to Jesus that we are automatically new creations who don't need to deal with past hurts.

It's certainly much easier to say, "Praise God, I'm victorious in Christ" and pretend everything is fine than it is to go through the hard work of allowing Him entrance into these hurts. We've so well compartmentalized and pushed them down into the dark crevices of our hearts that it's just not that easy to access them.

So what do we do?

Go to church with our happy face on and keep people at arm's length, believing we're the only one feeling the way we do—the shame of it all turning us into a silent victim. After all, often times the church isn't a safe place to admit our pain and struggles, so it's just easier to wear a mask and suffer in silence.

## How Does Jesus Bring Healing?

In Jesus's conversation with the woman at the well, He modeled how He brings healing to those of us who are wounded. After He spoke the unedited and unvarnished truth about her life and multiple husbands, He called her into vibrant faith . . . faith that faced the truth, no matter how painful, by the power of the Holy Spirit.

But the time is coming—indeed it's here now—when true worshipers will worship the Father in spirit and in truth. The Father is looking for those who will worship him that way. For God is Spirit, so those who worship him must worship in spirit and in truth. (John 4:23–24 NLT)

Notice He said that those who worship Him *must* worship in spirit and in truth. That doesn't sound like a suggestion or a recommendation, but a command. This is the only way to find the healing we are looking for. Jesus invites her to be a true worshiper . . . and He is inviting us to be the same:

- Honest about our pain, coming out of denial and into truth. (Psalm 38:4–8)
- Open to facing our wounds and seeing His purpose in our pain. (2 Corinthians 1:34)
- Near to His heart about our unhealthy response to trauma. (Psalm 103:14)
- Earnest in our repentance, receiving His cleansing (Psalm 51:1–3)
- Secure in our forgiveness, from Him, for the one who sinned against us, and for ourselves. (Matt. 6:12)
- Trusting Him for our healing. (Psalm 147:3)

One thing I know about our heavenly Father—He never wastes our pain. He uses it to grow us, to refine us, and to show us His love for us, enabling us to turn around and comfort others in their pain. His heart is to always, always, always bring good out of the pain in our lives. That's a promise.

### Resilient Truth

And we know that in all things God works for the good of those who love him, who have been called according to his purpose. (Romans 8:28 NLT)

His heart is to always, always, always bring good out of the pain in our lives. That's a promise.

## Resilient Prayer

*Almighty God,* only You could take a regretful, horrible, and devastating decision to end the life of my child and use it to minister hope to others who have suffered just as I have suffered. Thank You for healing my damaged emotions, and thank You in advance for bringing good out of the tragedies in my life. In Jesus's name. Amen.

## Resilient Action

Look up all the Scripture verses in the HONEST acrostic on page 117. Which ones speak to you the most clearly? Below, list three steps you can take to move toward the healing Jesus wants to work in your heart.

_____

_____

_____

_____

_____

Athena Dean Holtz serves as the publisher at Redemption Press. Her memoir, *Full Circle: Coming Home to the Faithfulness of God*, tells her story of overcoming severe spiritual abuse. Past president of the Northwest Christian Writers' Association, former radio host of *Always Faithful*, and host of the *All Things Podcast*, she is married to Dr. Ross Holtz, founding pastor of The Summit in Enumclaw, Washington.

## Chapter Seventeen

*Hiding*

B. J. Garrett

I don't want to be a father.

"What?" I whispered. This was not what I had expected. In an instant my excitement turned to shock and devastation. Immediately I sucked in all my emotion.

"How far along are you?" he asked.

"Four weeks. I just found out."

"I don't want you to have that baby."

My father's drunken words came back to me. *I wish you had never been born.* They hurt as much now as they had then. Many times in my childhood, I, too, had wished I had never been born. All I could think was that I would never let an unwanted child be born into what I had been born into. I could not—I would not—bring this baby into a home where he or she was not wanted, plain and simple.

"Okay," I said. "I'll make an appointment for an abortion."

The decision to abort my child that hot Texas summer day quickly caused destruction in my heart and soul that mirrored the flames of hell lapping the lost souls and that tormented me constantly. There were no takebacks in the abortion world. Already that "quick fix" was turning into a lifelong wound, never to be forgotten. A void so heavy with the weight of loss, that I was sure I could not even get out of bed many days.

Like so many others I believed I was the only one hurting this badly. The emotional turmoil caused havoc in my mind and in my heart. The emptiness of my womb was a physical representation of how my heart felt . . . desolate. I struggled for over a decade, believing I was the only one hurting this way.

If abortion solved my problem, why did my relationship end? Why was my world turned completely inside out more than a decade later? Why did I hurt so badly? And why would I make this choice again later in life, knowing how badly it hurt the first time? Why the nightmares, depression, and the string of emotional and spiritual complications I now battle daily?

In the pro-life world, Psalm 139:13–14 is quoted more than any other Scripture. And for good reason. We want moms to realize that despite the challenging or scary circumstances surrounding their pregnancies, their child is a gift from the Lord and is being knit together in their womb. Unfortunately, this Scripture can also feel like a spiritual slap in the face to those who have already chosen abortion.

Yes, it is very true. I know my children were knit together and that they were created by God. Out of fear and selfishness, I took those lives, and recognizing this truth caused so much chaos within my heart. Why would a loving, baby-knitting God ever love me after what I'd done?

You see, there is more to that Bible passage, but I was hung up on applying it only to my children I'd lost to abortion. You must take in all of that passage and apply it personally. I too was wonderfully made, and not one day of my life was a secret to Him, even while I was in my mother's womb. He never left me when I chose the dark path of abortion, nor was He surprised by my choice. Psalm 139:1–16 (NIV) says,

I too was wonderfully
made, and not one day of
my life was a secret to
Him, even while I was in
my mother's womb.

You have searched me, Lord,
  and you know me.
You know when I sit and when I rise;
  you perceive my thoughts from afar.
You discern my going out and my lying down;
  you are familiar with all my ways.
Before a word is on my tongue
  you, Lord, know it completely.
You hem me in behind and before,
  and you lay your hand upon me.
Such knowledge is too wonderful for me,
  too lofty for me to attain.
Where can I go from your Spirit?
  Where can I flee from your presence?
If I go up to the heavens, you are there;
  if I make my bed in the depths, you are there.
If I rise on the wings of the dawn,
if I settle on the far side of the sea, even there your hand will guide me,
  your right hand will hold me fast.
If I say, "Surely the darkness will hide me
  and the light become night around me,"
even the darkness will not be dark to you;
  the night will shine like the day,
  for darkness is as light to you.
For you created my inmost being;
  you knit me together in my mother's womb.
I praise you because I am fearfully and wonderfully made;
  your works are wonderful;
  I know that full well.
My frame was not hidden from you
  when I was made in the secret place,
  when I was woven together in the depths of the earth.

He never
left me when
I chose the
dark path
of abortion,
nor was He
surprised by
my choice.

Your eyes saw my unformed body;
all the days ordained for me were
written in your book
before one of them came to be.

I feel like I relate so much to the woman at the well referred to in John 4:6–42. This woman had big, fat ugly sin all over her. She was so broken and ashamed that she'd waited until the absolute hottest part of the day to go get water from the well so that she could be certain that no one would be there. She knew the looks of disgust she would garner and the cruel words that were spewed her direction when others saw her. So she hid in shame, only venturing out when she was most certain all others would be long gone.

The same woman who moments before had avoided all contact with others is now running around town, telling everyone about Jesus. Her shame no longer her bondage. She was free.

But then she met Jesus, and when Jesus asked her to go call her husband to join them at the well, she hid her secret, lied, and said, "I have no husband." Jesus reminded her she had five husbands and that the man she was living with was not her husband.

But instead of condemnation, she was told about the good news, forgiveness for her mistakes, and the chance for a new life if she believed the truth of who she had just met—Jesus, the Messiah, her salvation.

Is that you? Are you so burdened with your shame and brokenness that you attempt to avoid all human contact? Do you feel the unspoken judgment from the mere glances of others, thinking that if they knew all you have done, they would never even allow themselves to be in the same room with you?

If like me and the woman at the well, this describes your shame, can I encourage you to break through these lies from the Enemy? His power over you and your silence is only crippling you. Satan does not want you to have freedom. Especially if he has already lost your soul, he needs to be sure you are silenced.

Later in John 4, after the woman has an encounter with our loving Savior, she runs to the people of the town and tells them all about this amazing man who just changed her life for all of eternity. The same woman who moments before had avoided all contact with others is now running around town, telling everyone about Jesus. Her shame no longer her bondage. She was free. And she could not keep it to herself, and because she could no longer hide in the secret, her entire town gets saved!

Does this mean you need to run to the city square and tell your whole town of your loss through abortion? No. But I do hope it encourages you to seek out trustworthy, Jesus-loving friends to begin telling your secret. Run to Jesus with your secret. Instead of running from Him, attempting to hide your sin and pain, run to Him who is the only One who has the power to forgive, heal, and restore.

## Resilient Truth

He heals the brokenhearted and binds up their wounds. (Psalm 147:3 NIV)

## Resilient Prayer

*Dear Heavenly Father,* help me to trust You with my pain. Help me to run to You instead of away from You. Please put opportunities in my path to experience Your healing power in my life and to use my story as a tool to help others know Your forgiving grace. In Jesus's name. Amen.

> Run to Jesus with your secret. Instead of running from Him, attempting to hide your sin and pain, run to Him who is the only One who has the power to forgive, heal, and restore.

 *Resilient Action*

Look at Psalm 139:1–16 and write it out, inserting your name every place it uses the word "I" and "me." Then read it out loud as a prayer back to God and thank Him that He is the one who knows you intimately and loves you with a perfect, unconditional love.

B. J. Garrett released her memoir, *Unwanted No More,* in 2019. She serves as the executive director for Christ-Centered Abortion Recovery & Education and holds an associate of divinity degree from Baptist Missionary Theological Seminary. BJ has served in church ministries as a youth director, singles director, missions director, and women's ministry team leader. She and her husband, Jay, live in Texas and enjoy spending time with their children and grandchildren.

## Chapter Eighteen

## To the Wounded Girl Inside

### Andrea Tomassi

If you only knew.

Sweet girl, I know you are ashamed of the choice you made to abort your unborn child. I wish you had someone back then you felt you could trust. I am so sorry you had to go through this all alone. I wish you knew what grace looked like. Because if you did, you wouldn't have spent thirty years living with guilt and shame. If only I had fully known you. If I had, these are some truths found in God's Word I would have shared with you to make absolutely certain you understood your rightful inheritance in the family of God.

You are deeply loved, precious one. Do you realize there is nothing that can ever separate you from God's perfect love? (Romans 8:38). Not the decisions you've made or the steps you don't take. There is *nothing* you could ever say or do that will change God's view of you.

You don't need to do anything for God to love you.

His grace is sufficient for you.

He loves you just the way you are.

You don't need to perform better, work harder, or try to be the best at everything. Sadly, this will be a character defect you will carry into adulthood. You will

He is a gracious, loving, compassionate Father who longs to bring hope, healing, and wholeness to your life.

determine the basis of love from others by how well you perform, and you will struggle most of your adult life with perfectionism.

God saved you by his grace when you believed. And you can't take credit for this; it is a gift from God. Salvation is not a reward for the good things we have done, so none of us can boast about it. (Ephesians 2:8–9 NLT)

I know you believe God is a punishing God—He is not! He is a gracious, loving, compassionate Father who longs to bring hope, healing, and wholeness to your life. He is not going to send fire down from heaven to strike you, and He does not hate you. He has forgiven you and sees you as holy and perfect because of the sacrifice He made when He gave up his only Son for the decisions and mistakes you've made. You are still the apple of His eye, His precious and beautiful daughter. It breaks my heart that you never saw yourself this way.

> For the honor of your name, O Lord,
>    forgive my many, many sins.
> Who are those who fear the Lord?
>    He will show them the path they should choose,
> they will live in prosperity,
>    and their children will inherit the land.
> The Lord as a friend to those who fear him,
>    he teaches them his covenant.
> My eyes are always on the Lord,
>    for he rescued me from the traps of my enemies.
> Turn to me and have mercy,
>    for I am alone and in deep distress.
> My problems go from bad to worse,
>    Oh, save me from them all!

Feel my pain and see my trouble.
Forgive all my sins. (Psalm 26:11–18 NLT)

You don't need to carry guilt and shame inside of you. The condemnation you feel is not from God. You are forgiven. Don't you know you are a *new* creation in Christ? You are not defined by the choices you have made. They are thoughts put into action. It is not a reflection of who you are.

> Therefore, if anyone is in Christ, he is a new creation. The old has passed away; behold, the new has come. (2 Corinthians 5:17 ESV)

> There is therefore now no condemnation for those who are in Christ Jesus. (Romans 8:1 ESV)

I know you don't believe this right now, but you will not always feel this way. With age, you will grow wiser, stronger, and closer to God with each passing year. You will grow in your faith and learn to lean on Him for everything. He will be your Savior, your best friend, your provider, your husband, your deliverer. There will be seasons in your life when you feel alone, like He's not listening. But please know this: in those desolate seasons, He never left you, not for one second. He will always be right beside you, fighting for you. You must remember to trust in the truth you *know* and not place your trust in what you feel. Your feelings are ever changing, but God's Word stands true forever. "Do not be afraid or discouraged, for the Lord will personally go ahead of you. He will be with you; he will neither fail you nor abandon you" (Deuteronomy 31:8 NLT).

Rejoice, my sister. God will use for good everything the Enemy sent to destroy you! He will turn around the wrong choice you have made and give you a second chance. Everyone that has tried to harm you, every unfair circumstance, every wrong decision you've made,

He will turn around the wrong choice you have made and give you a second chance. . . He will turn all of it into something beautiful.

and each unkind word that has ever been spoken over you—He will turn all of it into something beautiful. Ultimately, to bring Himself glory and to show the world who holds the victory.

> Dear friends, don't be surprised at the fiery trials you are going through, as if something strange were happening to you. Instead, be very glad—for these trials make you partners with Christ and his suffering, so that you will have the wonderful joy of seeing his glory when it is revealed to all the world. (1 Peter 4:12–13 NLT)

You don't even know it yet, but you will make a difference in the lives of so many people. One day you will share this story of shame and regret and tell the world how Jesus is a healer and restorer. For you are chosen and precious in our Father's sight. He is so proud of the woman you will become. You will overcome many obstacles and trials in your life, and with each chapter you will birth a beautiful redemption story. You will walk in obedience and strive to do what is right out of reverence for Christ all the days of your life.

> You did not choose me, but I chose you and appointed you that you should go and bear fruit and that your fruit should abide, so that whatever you ask the Father in my name, he may give it to you. (John 15:16 ESV)

Precious girl, you are enough! You are worthy of everything good and right in this world. You deserve love and honor. You are important and you matter. I know loving yourself is a struggle. Take heart—you will learn how to love yourself when you are much older, but it will always be a struggle. I wish you understood the power in placing your hope and trust in Christ. When you put your hope in anything else, it's a recipe for disaster. You will discover God's love is the *only* thing you can never lose.

If the creator of the universe can forgive you, don't you think it's time to forgive yourself?

I know you can't go back and change the choices you've made, but if the creator of the universe can forgive you, don't you think it's time to forgive yourself? Isn't it time to release the burden of shame and regret? You've carried this for far too long. It has been a heavy weight that you were never meant to carry, and it will affect the decisions you make in the future.

Fill her precious heart with Your mercy and grace so that she may offer it to herself as well.

Take it to the foot of the cross, dear one. He's been waiting for you with arms open wide.

He sees you.

He's forgiven you.

He loves you.

He knows.

 *Resilient Truth*

You intended to harm me, but God intended it all for good. He brought me to this position so I could save the lives of many people. (Genesis 50:20 NLT)

*Resilient Prayer*

*Father, I pray* for the girl reading my story today. I pray that she, too, would come to a place of healing and redemption. Not from anything she can do on her own, but only from our true restorer God, and that's You! Fill her precious heart with Your mercy and grace so that she may offer it to herself as well. I pray she walks with You closely all the days of her life, knowing she is Your precious one. In Jesus's name. Amen.

 ## Resilient Action

If you are this girl and you have carried the same burden of shame along with the feeling of never being good enough, I would encourage you to write the same kind of letter you've just read. Add Scriptures that crush the lies you have believed for far too long. Then share the letter with a close friend or someone you trust. We are only as sick as our secrets. I know for some of you reading this, you've never told anyone your secret. I can't encourage you enough to share this with someone. You don't have to walk out your story alone.

_____

_____

_____

_____

_____

_____

Andrea (Andi) Tomassi is the author of the award-winning *Live Bold: A Devotional Journal to Strengthen Your Soul* devotional. She founded Transcended Ministries, inspiring women to rise above their circumstances and claim their identity in Christ. She believes no hurt is ever wasted and longs to bring a message of hope as she shares resilient stories of bold faith.

# Part 4

# Depression and Anxiety

## Chapter Nineteen

## *Everything Is Everything*
### Dr. Saundra Dalton-Smith

At the times of my deepest despair, friends would encourage me to trust God. Trusting God is difficult when everything you see appears to be in direct rebuttal to the promises shared in His Word. But when I allow God to break me free from my limited perspective, He reveals the depth and magnitude of His loving plan to bring me into His best. When I go against the pull of my emotions and dare to move beyond mere religion to relationship, a door is opened to move in the sacred space of living as His beloved. The passage through this door requires an honest answer to the question: Can I trust God with everything? A question I struggled to answer because I did not.

I spent many years bartering with God over which aspects of my life I would willingly surrender. He could have my career but not my children. I could trust Him with my past emotional pain but not my marriage. After many attempts to keep some level of power, I came to the conclusion that He wants to reign over it all. Everything in my life, everyone I love, every aspect of who I am. And no matter how much I love or treasure a person or situation, everything is everything. There is no partial trust. Either you choose to trust God, or you don't. And if you don't, then where was trust severed? When did you feel like He failed you?

For me trust was severed very early in my life. Growing up I can recall on numerous occasions crying out to God, asking why my mother had to die in childbirth. I found it incomprehensible to believe in God's faithfulness when it seemed as if He had snatched away the most important person in my life before I could even meet her. This level of severed trust cast a haze of doubt over my relationship with God for most of my adult life, until I had children of my own.

As a young married woman, I found myself longing for children with a deep ache that can only be appreciated by those who have had a period of barrenness. Despite how hard we tried, a baby did not appear to be in God's plan for our life. If you've been there, then you are familiar with the smile that has to be forced on your lips as friend after friend informs you of their pregnancy.

One night I resigned my desire to be a mother and said I would love God even if I never had children of my own. One month later I was showing the double blue lines to my husband as we cried in the living room together. Surrender both closes and opens—closing off the power of my fears and opening a place for faith to arise.

Pregnancy was both a blessing and a time of personal trial. Medically, no one could answer the question about what led to my mother's death in childbirth, so for many in my family, there was a level of apprehension around the time of my due date.

Those nine months went by quickly, and before I knew it, I found myself in a hospital labor and delivery suite. Hours after my epidural was administered, I experienced an acute reaction to the medication, which led to a stream of people running into the room. I could see fear gripping those around me, and for the first time I believe my husband contemplated the thought, *What would I do with a baby and no wife?* Moments later I felt a familiar jab deep within my womb, as if my son was telling me all was well, as the anesthesia was reversed and the fetal monitors all returned to healthy patterns. I could also feel God's presence in the room, reversing years of emotional baggage, pulling down generations of pain to bring forth new life.

Are there areas of your life where trust is

> Surrender both closes and opens— closing off the power of my fears and opening a place for faith to arise.

hard? How can one trust God after learning your child has leukemia or your home is being foreclosed? Trust can be severed over a job lay-off or the death of a loved one. It can be severed over a missed opportunity or a closed door of advancement.

Is there any part of your life that you do not want infused with God's power and blessing?

The list of trust-severing disappointments is as varied as the stars in the sky, but the outcome is always the same. Distance. It is that distance that makes moving forward with God impossible. It is in that place of severed trust where you learn about the areas of your life that you cling to as off limits to God. Off limits to God means off limits to all He is capable of bringing to the situation. No restoration, no redemption, no grace, no mercy, no peace, no joy, no hope.

Is there any part of your life that you do not want infused with God's power and blessing? I still to this day have to regularly do a quick check of my emotions to decipher which areas I've reclaimed as mine. I just as quickly render it all back to His capable hands. It's that easy. No, actually, it is never easy—you just have to choose to do it. It is never easy to release control of all you love and treasure, because even in our limited relationship with eternity, a part of us still likes to think we ultimately control our own destiny. Trust is not easy, but it is a choice worth pursuing daily.

My parenting journey was the start of a new era of learning how to trust God with everything. Motherhood showed me just how little I knew. Every new milestone was a step into the unknown, and with each step the fears mounted. Worry became my daily dwelling place, as I desperately tried to help God be God. I soon found myself in need of a new way of looking at religion's role in my life. I needed to shift from my need to control to simply delighting in God.

Psalm 37:4–6 (NKJV) tells us to

> Delight yourself also in the Lord,
>   And He shall give you the desires of your heart.
>  Commit your way to the Lord,
>    Trust also in Him,
>  And He shall bring it to pass.

He shall bring forth your righteousness as the light,
And your justice as the noonday.

My attempts to control things only left me depressed, exhausted, disappointed, disillusioned, and overwhelmed. My life lacked joy, peace, and fulfillment—the fruit produced when I delight myself in the Lord. The reward is not in expecting God to give me everything I want but that my heart will be aligned with His will. It is a repositioning under His grace and mercy over my life. It's an opportunity to commit and submit. An opportunity to trust the journey even when I do not know the way or the outcome. He alone is responsible for bringing forth any righteousness and any justice to be given. He alone is the greatest reward.

One of my fondest memories as a mom is playing the How Much game with my boys. Tiny toes would peek out from the bottom of their pj's as they stood barefoot in front of me as I asked, "How much does Mama love you?" They'd hold up fingers only inches apart as I'd say, "Nope, more than that." Next they'd hold up hands a foot apart. "No, even more." Finally, they'd stretch their arms wide, pointing from east to west. "Yes!" I'd exclaim. "I love you that much!"

One night after tucking them in to sleep, on the walk back to my bedroom I sensed God asking me a similar question. *How much do you trust me?* Tears ran down my face because for the first time in my life I could stretch my arms wide and declare, "This much, Lord."

 *Resilient Truth*

But my trust is in you, O Lord; you are my God. (Psalm 31:14 GNT)

*Lord,* thank You for Your loving kindness toward me. In every season, Your faithfulness has been evident. Help me to see Your goodness even during the times when the circumstances didn't look good. Show me how to turn my cares and concerns over into Your capable hands. Reveal anything that I hold more valuable than You. Give me the courage to surrender all. When I struggle to trust, draw me near and guide my heart. May my soul find its delight in You. Lead me in the direction of Your best for my life.

How much do You trust me? Tears ran down my face because for the first time in my life I could stretch my arms wide and declare, "This much, Lord."

 *Resilient Action*

What areas of your life do you struggle to trust God? Write down each area, and beside it write down your greatest heart's desire in that area. Instead of rehearsing your fears, spend time in prayer lifting up your petitions. What are ways you can delight yourself in the Lord today?

Dr. Saundra Dalton-Smith is a board-certified physician, popular speaker, and award-winning author of *Sacred Rest*, *Come Empty*, and *Set Free to Live Free*. She shares biblical truths to help heal the body, mind, and spirit. She transparently shares how her past pain has been redeemed through the practical application of God's Word. Learn more at IChooseMyBestLife.

Chapter Twenty

## Why Do I Feel This Way?
by Cynthia Cavanaugh

Angry, frustrated, and confused, I boarded a plane for Southern California. My husband's mother lay in a hospital bed with the shadow of death hovering. Unlike many in-law relationships, ours was different. She'd welcomed me to the family with both arms and a generous heart that forever changed the definition of the word "mother-in-law." I was devastated that we were about to lose her.

As I sat on the plane numb and expressionless, I cried, "Lord, where are you? I wanted to scream, "LORD, I CAN'T DO THIS ANYMORE!" I felt as though God's face were shrouded from me.

This is one of the few times in my journey with God where I truly felt abandoned. Multiple traumatic events had happened in a short period. Two weeks earlier, my family had buried our grandfather—our spiritual rock. I had the privilege of caring for and walking with him through his last days. Now, just weeks after his death, I was possibly facing another. Months later, my aunt died of cancer. A short time after, we moved to a new country and changed jobs, which brought upheaval to my family.

My dark journey began earlier that spring when I was diagnosed with clinical depression. The long days and weeks of caregiving for my grandfather took its toll. Blackness and despair sought to submerge me. The diagnosis of depression was

Blackness and despair sought to submerge me. The diagnosis of depression was difficult for my pride to digest. I could swallow a diagnosis of arthritis or diabetes, but depression? In my mind, depression was for weak people and feeble Christians who didn't seem to have enough faith. I argued about the diagnosis with God, my counselor, pastor, and doctor, all people who were trying to help me. "I am a visible leader, a pastor's wife in our church. What will people whisper about me behind closed doors if they know the truth?" Of course, these lies were causing me anxiety, and these lies kept me up at night.

My perspective shifted as my journey through depression continued over the next few years. As I swallowed my pride and allowed others to help me, I discovered my despair wasn't only from the losses I experienced, nor was it from my physical and emotional exhaustion. These were only warnings. Instead, it was, in part, from deeper issues tucked away for a long time—issues God brought to the surface. Issues such as false expectations and a warped perspective of needing to perform to feel loved. The lies destroyed me and plunged my spiritual and emotional being into the dark hole of depression. I started to see how performance gripped like a vice as a stronghold over my heart. With my counselor, I realized the depression was a symptom of something deeper, something I needed to face to be a whole person.

As Christians, we often struggle alone because of the fear of rejection, failure, or being told, "If your faith is stronger, you wouldn't be depressed." (Believe it or not, I was told similar statements!) Unfortunately, and sad to say, the church hasn't always done an adequate job to encourage and support those who suffer from depression. There are probably as many reasons for this as there are complications and symptoms of depression. I thank God that in the past few years, the church has begun to acknowledge depression as an illness rather than veiwing it as a sign of weakness or spiritual failure, and yet we still we have a long way to go.

I look back on that season of my life and thank God for the healing and His faithfulness, even amid the darkness.

The road to wholeness was a rigorous journey for me, but God gently reminded me over and over again, "This too shall pass." In all, I suffered five dark years of clinical depression. Today, I look back on that season of my life and thank God for the healing and His faithfulness, even amid the darkness.

God gently reminded me over and over again, "This too shall pass."

Elijah became my companion as I wrestled with depression. His story of acknowledging his need for restoration as a result of despair is found in I Kings 19:1–8 (NLT):

> When Ahab got home, he told Jezebel what Elijah had done and that he had slaughtered the prophets of Baal. So Jezebel sent this message to Elijah: "May the gods also kill me if, by this time tomorrow, I have failed to take your life like those whom you killed."
>
> Elijah was afraid and fled for his life. He went to Beersheba, a town in Judah, and left his servant there. Then he went on alone into the desert, traveling all day. He sat down under a solitary broom tree and prayed that he might die. "I have had enough, Lord," he said. "Take my life, for I am no better than my ancestors." Then he lay down and slept under the broom tree. But as he was asleep, an angel touched him and told him, "Get up and eat!" He looked around and saw some bread baked on hot stones and a jar of water! So he ate and drank and lay down again. Then the angel of the Lord came a second time and touched him, "Get up and eat some more, for there is a long journey ahead of you." So he got up and ate and drank, and the food gave him enough strength to travel forty days and forty nights to Mount Sinai, the mountain of God.

Elijah was utterly exhausted after his great victory on Mount Carmel defeating the false prophets of Baal. He ran for his life and collapsed under a solitary broom tree. His statement "I have had enough Lord. Take my life, for I am no better than my ancestors" says it all and points to a severe emotional collapse.

Can you relate to our friend Elijah?

Is that your cry today "I have had enough Lord?"

*Once I collapsed into God's loving arms and surrendered to the valley, I could rest and allow God to touch the wounded and hurting parts of my soul.*

Whatever you are facing this day, whatever nightmare you have woken up to, let me assure you God is listening even if it feels like your prayers seem to bounce off the ceiling.

Look what God did for Elijah while he was asleep. He sent him an angel to make him breakfast—it happened twice!

So often I think when I collapse in exhaustion or weariness, God is standing there waiting to give me a good kick to get going. But God knows, as Psalm 103:14 says, "He knows our frame; he knows we are but dust." He understands our human frailty more than we know.

One of the keys to understanding your depression is to surrender to it. Yes, you heard me, right! Oh, how I fought the label of depression and the truth that I was suffering from chronic depression. But once I collapsed into God's loving arms and surrendered to the valley, I could rest and allow God to touch the wounded and hurting parts of my soul.

God isn't a cruel taskmaster, and He knows your depression is real. Tell Him what you need, and watch Him enter into your pain and give you comfort. I invite you to rest as Elijah did, under the broom tree. Rest in God's arms under your broom tree, your circumstances that have brought you to this place, and let the Creator God of the universe serve you breakfast!

 *Resilient Truth*

The Lord is near to the brokenhearted and saves the crushed in spirit. (Psalm 34:18 ESV)

*Lord in heaven,* how awesome you are, my hope, and my refuge. So much is happening, and it is hard to express. I don't know whether my emotions are up or down. Confusion seeks to reign over my heart and mind. I don't like being in this weak place. Help me not to listen to the lies of the Enemy, which shout, "You're a failure. You are ungodly. If you only prayed more or read your Bible often, you wouldn't be depressed." Jesus, I declare these are lies from the pit of hell.

God, I want to get well and have the dark cloud that is robbing me of my joy and health removed. Show me where I need to go to get help. Lord Jesus, help me to surrender my pride and not lose perspective. Help me to accept that it is okay not to be okay.

Rest in God's loving arms under your broom tree, your circumstances that have brought you to this place, and let the Creator God of the universe serve you breakfast!

Cynthia Cavanaugh ～

 *Resilient Action*

What do you need to surrender to accept your depression? How can you make a conscious choice to rest like Elijah? Make a list of what you can do to replenish your soul.

_____

_____

_____

_____

_____

_____

_____

_____

_____

_____

_____

_____

_____

Cynthia Cavanaugh is a speaker, life coach, and award-winning author of *Anchored: Leading Through the Storms* and *Live Bold: A Devotional Journal to Strengthen Your Soul*. She is the Strategic Marketing Coach for Redemption Press, and you can find her at www.cynthiacavanaugh.com, Facebook, and Instagram.

Chapter Twenty-One

## Getting Real to Heal
### Jodi Harris

The Pepto-Bismol-colored blanket draped my shoulders, my legs criss-crossed over the sterile hospital bed. My body racked with sobs of uncontrolled grief. Snot and tears ran down my face.

*Well, this is it. Ministry is over. No one will ever respect me as a leader again.* Depression got the best of me and threatened to take my life. Disappointment in who I'd become suffocated me.

*Pastors' wives aren't supposed to go through this. In fact, Christians aren't. We're supposed to have the joy of the Lord. What is wrong with me? I've been a Christian my whole life. I knew better*, I scolded myself.

Doing time in the mental hospital was humiliating. My pastor's-wife image was shattered, and I felt officially "crazy."

I'd hidden my pain and played my part: supportive spouse, nurturing mother, happy volunteer. My closest friends knew, my husband knew, but their encouragement and advice didn't help; it hurt. Well-meaning words and Scripture made me feel worse.

Two years earlier, my husband and I had moved from Southern California to the Bay Area to start a church. We loaded up our two young sons with our God-sized dreams, and the adventure began.

My husband went off to church plant each day, but I burped babies and washed countless piles of tiny laundry. *Thomas the Tank Engine* played on repeat while I fed, changed, and cleaned someone or something. Also on repeat. I was the walking dead, and my clothes reeked of rotten milk.

Each night Jeff told me about the people he'd met and the progress of our new church. I told him how many times someone threw up on me or pooped their pants and what color it was.

Motherhood was lonely. I missed my friends, my old church, my old life, and I just wanted my mom.

My God-sized dreams of co-planting were replaced with depression and heartache, desperation and disillusionment. Disappointment squeezed out new-motherhood joy.

As things got harder, so did marriage. My anger with God came out at my husband. I blamed them both for bringing me to this terrible place that looked nothing like the picture in my mind. I expected to raise my babies alongside new-mom friends, with time to participate in church ministry. But I wasn't making friends. I had no community. And no one to watch my babies so I could church plant.

*Did I misunderstand You, God? I thought You brought me here for ministry with my husband. It feels like You brought me out here in the wilderness to die, just like the Israelites. I'm alone with no one—I'm scared and sad and hate it so much.*

The joy of the Lord was *not* my strength. I had postpartum depression. And I just wanted to die.

Shame hovered. Prayers went unanswered. I was losing a battle I didn't know how to fight.

I couldn't fake fine any longer.

I was admitted to the hospital, where I spent the next two weeks alongside drug addicts, schizophrenics, and alcoholics. We were failures and outcasts by society's standards: weak, broken, and ashamed. No hiding here. Hospital patients can't pretend they're well.

As each person shared their story of deep pain and broken-

Through our confessions, our differences melted away, and our commonalities brought acceptance and healing.

ness, I watched the others come alongside with comfort and empathy, offering kind words, a touch, or silent acceptance of *you're not alone* and *me too*. No one gave advice. No one judged or critiqued wounds and bad decisions. Through our confessions, our differences melted away, and our commonalities brought acceptance and healing.

Of all places for God to show up. Among the weak and broken. The outcasts and sinners. The same place Jesus shows up in the New Testament. Go figure.

*Of all places for God to show up*, I thought. *Among the weak and broken. The outcasts and sinners. The same place Jesus shows up in the New Testament. Go figure.*

Why had I been so afraid of rejection for being broken and needing others' help? Why did I believe I was only as good as my behavior? As much as I loved Jesus, I believed lies of the Enemy: *You'll never be enough. You're a terrible mother and wife. God can't use you until you get your act together. If you were a real Christian, you wouldn't be depressed. As soon as people find out, your husband will lose his job. If Jesus really loved you, you'd be transformed by now. What's wrong with you?*

But here in this group, I realized the truth. "You guys!" I blurted out. "This is what the church is supposed to look like!" Many were not Christians, yet this wasn't an odd thing to hear from the resident pastor's wife. "If only Christians could feel accepted enough to admit their hurts and struggles. If only other Christians could *be* accepting enough to embrace those who confess. But in the church, we're afraid to admit we're broken. We think we're supposed to have it all together. But until we're willing to get real, we can't heal."

What I saw as the end was actually the beginning of my ministry and healing.

Since that day, in Scripture I've found a kindred spirit who also experienced a life-threatening battle. He too listened to lies of the Enemy. In his moment of despair, he cried out, and God saved him.

The next time the Enemy attacked, he responded differently.

In 2 Chronicles 20, when King Jehoshaphat gets word his enemies are attacking, he's afraid. I'm comforted by the fact that—even though God saved him before, he's still afraid. Because, me too.

But this time he goes straight to God. He gathers the people together and

> What I saw as the end was actually the beginning of my ministry and healing.

prays. In his prayer, he combats lies with truth. A God who

- rules over *all* nations with power and might no one can withstand,
- has driven out the enemy before, and
- hears them and will save them.

When I name truths of who God is, my thoughts shift from my weaknesses to God's strengths.

Next, the king confesses his fear.

Confession is freeing, isn't it? It's hard to give up our pride for sure, but I think God waits for us to admit our fears and need for help before He steps in.

As the king's prayer ends, they *wait in silence* for the Lord to answer. When I pray, I'm quick to move on and take charge of my day *without* God's input. I'm not good at sitting silently and listening expectantly to anyone, not even God. But how will He answer me if I give no space for Him to do so?

As the people wait, God answers them. And I'm pretty sure His plan looked nothing like what they would have come up with on their own: "Do not be afraid or discouraged because of this vast army. For the battle is not yours, but God's. . . . You will not have to fight this battle. Take up your positions; stand firm and see the deliverance the LORD will give you. The Lord will be with you" (2 Chronicles 20:15, 17 NIV).

What? Say that again? We don't have to fight? We just get to watch?

I love what happens next: the king and his people fall down *in worship* before the Lord. And *as they sing and praise*, the *Lord* defeats their enemy.

Their weapon was worship. And so is ours.

My battle with depression and anxiety is not over. The Enemy still attacks. But like a little child, when I feel afraid, I cry out to my Dad, Abba Father. I raise my hands in surrender and wait for Him to scoop me up and hold me close. As we sit together, I worship and praise, meditating on His truths about me as His kid, and He defends, heals, rescues, and protects.

I still ask God for complete healing from depression, but like the apostle Paul, I see my struggle as a gift:

> My grace is sufficient for you, for my power is made perfect in weakness. Therefore I will boast all the more gladly of my weaknesses, so that the power of Christ may rest upon me. For the sake of Christ, then, I am content with weaknesses, insults, hardships, persecutions, and calamities. For when I am weak, then I am strong. (2 Corinthians 12:9–11 ESV)

What if victory over our battles doesn't look how we think? What if physical healing *isn't* the victory God has for me? What if, instead, His victory is spiritual healing, continued transformation into Christlikeness?

As I left the hospital years ago, my church-planting ministry began. And no, it didn't look anything like I thought, in my own strength. It looked like me confessing my weakness and claiming God's victorious truths and transformation.

In my brokenness, I've never felt more whole.

## Resilient Truth

> Therefore, confess your sins to one another and pray for one another, that you may be healed. The prayer of a righteous person has great power as it is working. (James 5:16 ESV)

## Resilient Prayer

*Lord,* I have no power to face the enemy that is attacking me. I do not know what to do, but my eyes are on You. Thank You for fighting this battle. Thank You for being with me. Help me to stay focused on You and not the battle. The victory is Yours! (2 Chronicles 20:12, 15, 17)

As they sing and praise, the Lord defeats their enemy. Their weapon was worship. And so is ours.

 *Resilient Prayer*

Read 2 Chronicles 20:1–30.

1. Write down your current struggle and what you believe on one side of the page. On the other, write truths about who God is and what He's done.
2. Confess your fears and your struggles to God.
3. Sit in silence and wait for Him to speak. Write down anything that comes to you: thoughts, impressions, or Scripture God lays on your heart.
4. Worship—choose a few of your favorite worship songs to sing or listen to, or read out loud a psalm that speaks to you.
5. Repeat this practice as you wait on God.

_____

_____

_____

_____

_____

_____

_____

_____

As a Bible teacher, speaker, and writer, Jodi Harris is in passionate pursuit of Jesus and living a better story. She is contributing author to the books *Bloom Where You're Planted: Stories of Women in Church Planting, Volumes 1, 2, and 3*. Connect with her at justjodiharris.com, where she writes about life and struggles, Scripture, and the importance of coffee creamer.

## Chapter Twenty-Two

### Season of Silence
#### Lori Peters

"There is something wrong with your son." This is what I was hearing from my son's pediatrician on the other end of the phone. *Wait!* I had been asking doctor after doctor the past eighteen months about my son's delays and had only been brushed off as a hypersensitive first-time mom. "He's a boy; he'll catch up." That is what I was told time and time again. *Now* something is "wrong" with my son? This could not be true.

*Wait!*

I could not possibly have a child with special needs. That was crazy. I lived a good life. I was a good girl. I went to a Christian college. I went to seminary. I had committed to full-time ministry. Having played by the rules, I thought I should receive a blessing and fulfillment of a long-awaited dream.

I was completely numb. I did not even remember hanging up the phone. However, my denial did not last very long. My act-first-process-later intuition kicked in after about two days. I was online researching every specialist, doctor, and therapist. If there was something wrong with my son, I was going to correct it. The doctors and specialists could not agree on a diagnosis, but that did not stop me.

At that time autism was just gaining ground, and there were all kinds of labels and diagnosis. My son immediately began early intervention. I found the best treatments in the Washington, DC, area and moved in for weeks at a time with my cousin so I could commute every day with my son for treatment. I found the best therapists and used them to find local therapy providers. I was implementing special diets, getting chelation, and my boy even withstood seventy-five injections in one day to desensitize him from certain allergens.

I was told by the best of the best, "He is going to be just fine." But just to make sure, I called the elders of my church to pray over us. Of course, I was going to make sure God was in all of this while orchestrating everything here on earth. God would certainly provide for me the miracle I was asking for, wouldn't he? What better way for God to receive the glory than to heal my son. I would certainly shout it from the mountaintops and be the poster child for God's goodness and faithfulness.

I was assured that by the time my son reached about the age of six he would be developmentally caught up within normal limits. My eye was on the goal, and I would not fail.

Age six came, then seven, then eight, and those normal limits were not being met. I would tell God, "Okay, I am ready for that miracle. I am ready for the desire of my heart to be fulfilled. I've put a team of the very best of the best together. I just need you to do your part, and that time would be about now." But nothing changed.

And then *it* happened. I crashed and burned. For six solid years I'd done everything humanly possible to get to the goal, and I was no closer than I had been at the beginning. I prayed, I believed, I claimed verses, and yet my son was still his own unique self—and my hope left. I sat in desperation in his bedroom for hours one afternoon praying verse after verse, and still nothing. God was not listening to me. He went silent.

No one could fully understand the depth of pain I was feeling. I was given many verses in which to hold fast to. If one more person told me that God created special women to be mothers of special needs children, I was going to scream. My Jersey Girl was about to be unleashed. I had relied on that crazy combo of Irish/Jersey strength to get me through everything, but this time it failed.

Actually, God failed me, at least that was what my heart believed. Why wasn't He answering me? What had I done to deserve His silence and such deep pain? What did I do to be treated this way? I fell into a deep depression. I lost all belief to have a normal life. I lost all desire to be a mom. I lost all sight of God and His goodness, and I just wanted to sleep forever.

Through the quick intervention of friends and family, I was given the opportunity for treatment at a Christian counseling center. My presence caused a bit of a problem, as I was a counselor and could out-counsel many. But the program director agreed to take me on and lovingly challenged my thinking. He shed new light on several issues I was facing and pointed me back to a loving heavenly Father who heard every word, knew every emotion, felt the depth of my pain, and held every tear in the palm of His hand. He never left me, nor had He forsaken me.

I had trust issues. *Wait!* I *have* trust issues. (This was not a one-and-done experience.) I am a continual work in progress. I learned quickly the close partner of "lack of trust" is "need to be in control." I did not trust God to work out His plan in this situation—I only trusted myself and hence took complete control. I focused on my goal and stopped listening for His guidance and direction for His perfect plan. However, as many of us may know, in Jeremiah 29:11 we are promised God's plan to give us hope. "For I know the plans I have for you," declares the Lord, "plans to prosper you and not to harm you, plans to give you hope and a future" (NIV).

But sometimes understanding God's plan can be so hard and hope seems to be an unattainable feeling. When His plan is not clear and pain is involved, I have a hard time surrendering to it, especially when I believe He has gone silent. However, if we continue reading, we are told in verses 12–14, "Then you will call upon me and come and pray to me and I will listen to you. You will seek me and find me when you seek me with all your heart. I will be found by you." I went running ahead and left God behind. What I desperately needed was to find God in the midst of my turmoil and heartbreak—not run from Him.

I was so busy seeking doctors and therapists to

> I had trust issues. Wait! I have trust issues. I am a continual work in progress.

heal my son, I never acknowledged my pain, and I stopped seeking the One who truly held my heart, hope, and ultimately my healing. David writes in Psalm 69 (NIV), "Save me, O God, for the waters have come up to my neck. I sink in the miry depths, where there is no foothold. I have come into the deep waters; the floods engulf me. I am worn out calling for help; my throat is parched. My eyes fail, looking for my God."

My eyes are what failed, and I was drowning in desperation, and I did not even realize it. I did not want to feel the pain, so I never bothered to stop and look for God, for His strength, His direction, and ultimately His will. Dropping my eyes to the circumstances took my footing out from under me and left me in a state of hopelessness, despair, and ultimately in a deep state of depression.

In coming to grips with being diagnosed as clinically depressed, I needed to learn new strategies for dealing with my emotions. When given the option of fight or flight, I fight. I took off running without even understanding what I was feeling. I was just going to fix the "wrong." I learned to stop and feel the pain. I learned to name that which I was feeling and give legitimacy to my emotions. I was challenged to cry out to God those emotions and pain in order for Him to move in and renew my heart and mind.

David did the same in Psalm 69:29 (NIV), "But as for me, afflicted and in pain—may your salvation, God, protect me."

I prayed for God to search my heart and know my anxious thoughts, to reveal those beliefs that clouded trust and confidence in Him. He did step in, and the pleas of my anxious and troubled mind became calm. A peace washed over me, and the promises of God saturated my soul.

My pain eventually turned into praise. My distrust changed to confidence. My need for control turned into my need for ultimate dependence on the God who never fails. My heart was changed, reflecting the very words of David's Psalm 28:6–7 (NIV): "Praise be to the Lord, for he has heard my cry for mercy. The Lord is my strength and my shield; my heart trusts in him, and I am helped. My heart leaps for joy, and I will give thanks to him in song."

A peace washed over me, and the promises of God saturated my soul.

God is faithful. He never leaves us, and He always hears our cries. Being proactive and assertive is not wrong. God gave me the wiring to be a fierce advocate for my son. God chose not to change my circumstances; instead He changed me. I have surrendered to God, His timing, His plan. I have also learned to trust Him with my darkest of feelings, believing He will renew my spirit and keep my feet on solid ground. He will do the same for all His precious children, if we just let Him. If we run to Him.

> **God chose not to change my circumstances; instead He changed me.**

## Resilient Truth

But blessed is the one who trusts in the Lord, whose confidence is in him. They will be like a tree planted by the water that send out its roots by the stream. It does not fear when heat comes; its leaves are always green. It has no worries in a year of drought and never fails to bear fruit. (Jeremiah 17:7–8 NIV)

## Resilient Prayer

*Abba Father, faithful and always true,* I am swimming in a pool of emotions, and I feel so overwhelmed. I am scared and I am in pain. Remind me that You know my heart, that You know my mind, and that you are ready to replace my anxious thoughts with healing and peace. Please come and make your presence known to me. Assure my troubled heart that You are in control of all things and promise good in my life. Please help me to release the feelings that are not of You and instead replace them with Your truth so I might be set free. Bring me the confidence in You and You alone. You are my God, my strength, and my refuge. Thank You for loving me.

 *Resilient Action*

Are there emotions you are feeling but are afraid to name either the fear of shame or failure? Can you trust God to accept those feelings knowing He already knows what they are and is wanting to relieve you of their weight? Find a quiet place and ask God to search your heart for those emotions that are weighing you down. Write them down and confess each one to your loving Father and let Him give you peace that surpasses all understanding.

Lori Peters is a speaker, organizational and leadership consultant, counselor, freelance writer, and professor at George Washington University. She is an advocate for equal opportunities for people with special needs and takes graduate classes in her spare time. You can find her at lorijpeters.com or Facebook and Instagram.

## Chapter Twenty-Three

### Worthless

Caris Snider

Worthless.
    Useless.
    Hopeless.
    Purposeless.
    These are the words depression used to bind and imprison me on a daily basis. How could I begin to think life was no longer worth living? Despair and defeat were slowly changing me. No longer did it matter my title in business, the type of mother I had become, or that I was leading worship. None of those things could prepare me for the pit I was falling into. It was like one of those slow-motion falls you see in the movies. Screams echo all the way down, and yet no one hears them. When you finally hit the bottom, it is like being punched in the gut by a fifth-grade bully. Breathing and thinking clearly are no longer options. Fog is now what engulfs every move. Darkness grips you with fear as depression whispers in your ear, "You will never make it out alive. No one will save you. You are alone. You are mine."
    Lies in this moment become your truth.
    Depression was something I never believed was real. When people would

come to me for counseling about depression, I would not respond with the compassion of Jesus. My answers to these broken souls may sound familiar to you: "Pray harder"; "Try harder"; "Trust God more"; "Read your Bible more"; "Suck it up, buttercup."

I had no idea the mental anguish they lived in every day. Then I became depression's next victim. It came for me. It came to steal my life and rob me of my purpose, just like it does to millions of others. Though others lived in this troubled state, I was convinced I was alone. No chance anyone else believed the horrible things about themselves I rehearsed in my mind as the sun rose in the morning and set in the evening. Light in my eyes flickered. Hope was fading. Death was swooping in on the back of depression. It nearly won.

*But God* . . .

After a miscarriage, God's grace covered me like a warm blanket. Shivers were no longer running down my spine. Even though brokenness was still there, peace began to glue the pieces back together in the most beautiful way. It was as if God picked me up, placed me in His lap, and said the words He knew I needed to hear, "I'm not mad at you. You are not alone. I still have a great purpose for you."

The journey out of the pit of depression took longer than falling into the dark hole that surrounded me. Through the help of my doctor, counselor, and community of friends, God gave me a new song to sing. The prison walls came down, and thriving in life the way our heavenly Father intended became an option.

I often wondered, Did anyone from the Bible have troubling thoughts I wrestled with frequently? What example did they give us to overcome depression? Did God still use them even though this battle waged in their life?

God gave me a new song to sing. The prison walls came down, and thriving in life the way our heavenly Father intended became an option.

The book of Jeremiah is where I landed. Jeremiah is known as the weeping prophet. He lived a lonely and depressed life. He knew what it was like to feel despair, rejection, fear, and loss of purpose. The way he handles his misery may surprise you. One of his cries to God can be found in Jeremiah 20:7–18(NIV):

You deceived me, Lord, and I was deceived;
  you overpowered me and prevailed.
I am ridiculed all day long;
  everyone mocks me.
Whenever I speak, I cry out proclaiming
  violence and destruction.
So the word of the Lord has brought me
  insult and reproach all day long.
But if I say, "I will not mention His word
  or speak anymore in His name,"
His word is in my heart like a fire,
  a fire shut up in my bones.
I am weary of holding it in.
  indeed, I cannot.
I hear many whispering,
  "Terror on every side!
  Denounce him! Let's denounce him!"
All my friends
  are waiting for me to slip, saying,
"Perhaps he will be deceived;
  then we will prevail over him
  and take our revenge on him."
But the Lord is with me like a mighty warrior;
  so my persecutors will stumble and not prevail.
They will fall and be thoroughly disgraced;
  their dishonor will never be forgotten.
Lord Almighty, you who examine the righteous
  and probe the heart and mind,
let me see your vengeance on them,
  for to you I have committed my cause.
Sing to the Lord!
  Give praise to the Lord!

Even though
brokenness was
still there,
peace began to
glue the pieces
back together
in the most
beautiful way.

He rescues the life of the needy
  from the hands of the wicked.
Cursed be the day I was born!
  May the day my mother bore me not be blessed!
Cursed be the man who brought my father the news,
  who made him very glad, saying,
  "A child is born to you—a son!"
May that man be like the towns
  the Lord overthrew without pity.
May he hear wailing in the morning,
  a battle cry at noon.
For he did not kill me in the womb,
  with my mother as my grave,
  her womb enlarged forever.
Why did I ever come out of the womb
  to see trouble and sorrow
  and to end my days in shame?

Wow . . . he had it rough, friends! He felt deceived by the Lord. He battled with some of the same thoughts and despairing emotions you and I have felt. He also shows us transparency in his path to dealing with them.

Honesty was not a problem for Jeremiah! He let God know real quick what He was thinking and how He was feeling. His words may sound harsh, but they are real. Here God has called Jeremiah to be a prophet and speak His truth to the Israelites, and now he is living in a nightmare.

Being silent was an option for Jeremiah. Wearing a mask to cover it up would have been easier. When God's Word was burning in his heart like a fire, taking the easy way out would have burned him from within. Even in his lament, he remembered the Lord was with him like a mighty warrior. Jeremiah could not let go of the fact that God was on his side. He knew

> Even in his lament, he remembered the Lord was with him like a mighty warrior.

the creator of the universe could handle his authentic emotions and dreadful thoughts.

Telling God the truth did not mean the Lord would leave him. It just meant He would hold up the shield over Jeremiah and defend him in an even greater way. Just as God was on Jeremiah's side, He is on your side. God already knows what is going on in your heart and mind. If He can handle these words from Jeremiah, He will be able to hear what you need to say.

> Shouts of worship and anticipation of deliverance began to ring from his lips! He knew God was moving heaven and earth on his behalf.

Not only did Jeremiah confess, but he praised! Remembering God as his mighty warrior meant reminding himself of his Abba Father. Shouts of worship and anticipation of deliverance began to ring from his lips! The rescue mission for Jeremiah was in motion. He knew God was moving heaven and earth on his behalf.

Jesus is our rescuer and redeemer. God knew we would need help. By having an attitude of praise and thankfulness, it opens the window of hope to allow Him to come in and do what only He can do.

Did Jeremiah only have amazing days from this point on? No. In fact, we see just a couple of verses down that he is wondering why he was allowed to even be born.

What about you?

Can you relate to Jeremiah?

Do you ever wonder why you were born?

Do you ever doubt the purpose and calling you know God has placed on your life?

His struggle was real, but God continued to use Jeremiah. God continued to walk the path with him. He did not leave Jeremiah's side even when misery became great company for him. God's love never fails, and it will not fail you. His purpose for you is where no one else can walk.

Depression may have caused you great pain and despair. It may have convinced you to think that the plan for your life has ended. Actually, it is beginning in a different light. God wants to open your eyes to a new way of living. You no longer have to hide your emotions and thoughts behind steel bars. Sitting alone in torture

> God loves you,
> and He will make
> sure to place
> people in your
> path to hear you
> even if it's only
> a whimper you
> can exhale.

is no longer a life sentence.

Ask God to help you break through the walls with your groaning and weeping. Your Daddy God is listening.

Ask Him for help even though depression spews its lie that no one will care and no one will come. God loves you, and He will make sure to place people in your path to hear you even if it's only a whimper you can exhale. The Lord's compassion is new every morning. Allow it to restore hope where agony and torture live. He is ready and prepared to hear all the mess, to allow His message to restore your soul.

## Resilient Truth

Yet this I call to mind and therefore I have hope; Because of the Lord's great love we are not consumed, for his compassions never fail. They are new every morning; great is your faithfulness. I say to myself, "The Lord is my portion, therefore I will wait for him." (Lamentations 3:21–24 NIV)

## Resilient Prayer

*Daddy God,* I am awestruck by the love You have for me. Thank You for never leaving me or forsaking me. Even in my pain and despair, You are there. My soul has been downcast for so long. Never did I think the broken pieces could be put back together. Thank You for showing me the glimmer of hope I needed to see. Help me to remember that You are not mad at me, I am not alone, and I do still have a unique purpose no one else can fulfill.

Help me to no longer receive the lies that I am useless, worthless, helpless, and purposeless. God, I want to believe You are fighting for me, but I need You to help my unbelief. Show me those on my path who can help me. Holy Spirit, help me to unmask all the words I have been hiding in my heart for so long. Help me to take steps forward, be okay with the steps back, and to keep going knowing a new beginning is out there for me. In Jesus's name. Amen.

## Resilient Action

What do you need to be honest about with the Lord when it comes to depression? Do you need to confess, like Jeremiah, the anger and doubts you may have about God's plan for your life? What are some things you can begin to praise and thank God for now in your life, to see His rescue mission in motion for you? Make a list below of the doubts you have experienced and what you can praise God for as He restores your soul.

The Lord's compassion is new every morning. Allow it to restore hope where agony and torture live. He is ready and prepared to hear all the mess, to allow His message to restore your soul.

What are some things you
can begin to praise and
thank God for now in your
life, to see His rescue
mission in motion for you?

_____

_____

_____

_____

_____

_____

_____

_____

_____

_____

_____

_____

_____

Caris Snider is a speaker, worship leader, and author of *Anxiety Elephants: A 31 Day Devotional to Help Stomp Out Your Anxiety*. She is passionate about helping other women overcome depression and anxiety through sharing her story. You can find her at www.carissnider.com and @carissnider on Facebook and Instagram.

## Chapter Twenty-Four

# White-Knuckled Driver
## Lyndie Metz

For as long as I can remember, I have been afraid of driving on highways. I cannot ever recall a time that I felt safe while driving with semitrucks at blazing speeds. I did not know that this was abnormal. I thought all people were fearful, and this happened to be one of my fears.

As a child, I didn't fear riding in cars. At the age of sixteen years and one month, I was excited to get my driver's license, and to this day, I prefer to drive everywhere myself.

Since I was a kid, I've had miserable motion sickness that is only kept at bay if I'm behind the wheel. Obviously, I didn't discover that until I was of legal driving age, but now that I'm there, I don't intend to stop driving myself . . . ever. Though I may not be the best driver in the world, I can guarantee I am one of the worst passengers. Especially in recent years.

I can look back and see the glimpses of anxiety throughout my childhood, adolescence, and early adulthood, but when I got married and had babies, things drastically worsened. I was over thirty when I married, so by society's standards, time was ticking. For me, it took exactly that long to surrender to God's plan for my life, and I knew that one of the most important parts of my plan would be whom I would marry.

It's ironic that at the same time God was expanding my world in this new phase of being a newlywed (and not long after, a new mama), my fears took root. Before marriage and children, I hardly had a care in the world. In fact, my parents would probably tell you that I gave them reason to fear many times. Whether it was moving across the country to find out who God made me to be or traveling to remote villages across oceans to see how beautiful God made everyone, I know that more than they preferred, I gave them reason to fear, and I had none.

Fast-forward a few years and you will find a much different version. As a wife, I started to fear my husband's safety and his health. Then I started to fear my own. As a mom, my goodness, I researched everything. (Don't do that!) With new worries and anxieties, I experienced hurdles in my faith and crashed down on everyone. I didn't see it as a spiritual battle, but oh, it was.

With one baby, I was just gaining information about being a good mom. When the second baby arrived, I started having irrational fears. Now, if something happens to me, my husband is left with two, not just one, and he's outnumbered. I never once traced this worry back to the terrified driver who couldn't just keep her eyes on the solid yellow line as trucks flew by.

After the third baby busted on the scene, I was having daily pep talks with myself. I worried when my children were away from me. I worried when they were home. If my husband was five minutes later than I expected, I feared the worst, *always*. The relief I experienced when he picked up the phone was indescribable. And it wasn't just my husband—it was my parents well-being that had the same fear-triggering effect on my mental and emotional state. I couldn't explain it. I didn't understand it. I felt helpless.

Do not fear, for I am with you; do not be afraid, for I am your God. I will strengthen you; I will help you; I will hold on to you with my righteous right hand.

The Bible has a lot to say about fear and anxiety. In fact, if you read the entire book, you will find that every book reassures us of God's presence and protection. Isaiah 41:10 (csb) says, "Do not fear, for I am with you; do not be afraid, for I am your God. I will strengthen you; I will help you; I will hold on to you with my righteous right hand." God's right hand is righteous. It always is. His right hand signifies special placement throughout the Bible. We are cared for, set apart, special, and yet when we go through trials in life, it can be difficult to keep that in mind.

Not too long ago I had a medical scare that put a spotlight on my anxiety. After dealing with major drama in a couple of areas of my life, my body was run down and desperate for attention. I went to work, as normal, but midmorning I felt shaky and was seeing spots. I looked down at my smartwatch to find that my heart rate was way higher than normal. The work I was in at the time had a perk I had taken for granted until that day. I was an elementary school teacher for the first decade of my adult life, and having the school nurse on call for immediate care and advice was much appreciated. She was able to calm me down and encourage me to see my primary care physician right away.

When I arrived at the doctor's office, I didn't know what to expect, but after a few different people visited me, I had my first echocardiogram of my life, and I found out that I had had a panic attack at work. Immediately, 1 Peter 5:7 (csb) ran through my mind: "Casting all your cares on him, because he cares about you."

Why on earth would someone who knows and loves God and believes wholeheartedly in His protection have a panic attack? A panic attack is the onset of fear, accompanied by the exact same physical symptoms I was exhibiting earlier that day. I had unresolved fear. I had not carried my worries to the cross and laid them down. I don't know about you, but sometimes I can carry my worries to the cross and not lay them down.

Proverbs 12:25 (csb) lets us know that "anxiety in a person's heart weighs it down." And the remedy for that is found in Philippians 4:6–7 (csb), "Don't worry about anything, but in everything, through prayer and petition with thanksgiving, present your requests to God. And the peace of God, which surpasses all understanding, will guard your hearts and minds in Christ Jesus."

I would love to wrap this story up with a nice, frilly bow and tell you that I got it that day, that all of my anxiety went away and I no longer had to deal with physical symptoms of worrying. That's just not true. As real as God makes Himself to

> I found comfort in knowing that no matter what, God is holding on to me with His righteous right hand.

me on a daily basis, Satan still tries to take ownership of my mind and heart by placing thoughts of worry and doubt. The good thing for you and me is that we know who wins, right?

I recently had another panic attack, but this time I was armed with information. I knew what was happening. That didn't stop me from freaking out and wondering if I was experiencing some other medical condition that needed urgent care. This time, though, I found comfort in knowing that no matter what, God is holding on to me with His righteous right hand.

I did follow up with my doctor, and if you suffer from anything that I have described thus far, I recommend you talk with your doctor. Here's why: God has given you access to great care with cutting-edge technology. Please use all of that for good. If you are troubled by something, don't self-diagnose by reading everything you can find online—that will likely worry you more. Not only can we find the peace that surpasses all understanding when we take our cares to God, but we can find the peace that comes from medical professionals giving us their best advice. Seek help if you need it.

And finally, remember the Good Shepherd of Psalm 23 (csb):

> The Lord is my shepherd;
> I have what I need.
> He lets me lie down in green pastures;
> He leads me beside quiet waters.
> He renews my life;
> He leads me along the right paths
> for his name's sake.
> Even when I go through the darkest valley,
> I fear no danger,
> for you are with me;
> your rod and your staff—they comfort me.
> You prepare a table before me

in the presence of my enemies;
you anoint my head with oil;
my cup overflows.
Only goodness and faithful love
will pursue me
all the days of my life
and I will dwell in the house of the lord
as long as I live.

## ~ Resilient Truth

Do not fear, for I am with you; do not be afraid, for I am your God. I will strengthen you; I will help you; I will hold on to you with my righteous right hand. (Isaiah 41:10 csb)

## ~ Resilient Prayer

*Father God,* We seek You. We need You. We are desperate for You. Lord, when the troubles of this life cause anxiety in our hearts, please remind us of Your Word, which gives us the remedies for our troubles. Remind us to pray and petition and be thankful for all that you have done for us. Help us to present our requests to You and leave them there. Give us peace, and guard our hearts and minds in Christ Jesus. Thank You for Your saving grace and Your unending love for us. We love You and thank You. In Jesus's name. Amen.

Only goodness and faithful love will pursue me all the days of my life:

 *Resilient Action*

1. How have you handled the anxieties and worries of life?
2. How might you be able to carry your fears to the cross and leave them there?

Lyndie Metz is an author and speaker with interests in Christian living, biblical application, and self-help. Her books *Be Still: Memoirs of a Motherless Daughter* and *A Seamless Life* recently hit shelves, and she loves connecting with her audience. You can connect with her at www. lyndiemetz.com or follow her @lyndie.l.metz on Facebook and Instagram.

# Part 5

# Betrayal

## Chapter Twenty-Five

### Done

#### Tammy Whitehurst

There comes a time when we are done.

Done with crying.

Done with anger.

Done with betrayal.

Done with bitterness.

Flat out . . . *done*.

It's like a slow cooker finally boiling over.

Most days I wake up smiling, put on my armor, and with humor bob and weave my way through whatever life throws at me. Most of my life has been lived this way. My goal is to seek the sunshine and happy things waiting to be found, which is not always easy. Then something happened.

Here's how it all began . . .

I woke up and had an ugly enemy bombarding me from all directions. It was all I could do not to weep helplessly. The one thing I want is to live life fully alive, and being bitter was like sinking in quicksand one slow suffocating moment at a time.

I was always told I was a good mother. At school, my students would told me they wished I was their mother. I loved big and hugged hard. I thought I had done things right.

As a child, I grew up in a big and happy family. A family that stuck together, valued our elders, laughed, and cried on one another's shoulders. No matter what we did, good or bad, silly or serious, we loved each other. God gave me these people to call mine forever, and I took it seriously. They are my people. Of course we had our hardships, tears and fears, but we always could stand up and brush ourselves off and keep going. We loved regardless.

Then without much warning, a bomb hit, and emotional shrapnel flew everywhere. My child walked away from the family. But most of all from me. I felt betrayed.

She'd served as my sidekick on mission trips because she was a fearless leader. I'd laughed with her and cried with her. I'd cheered her on and encouraged her through tough days. Then she went away to college, and the unthinkable happened. She not only left home, it felt as if she left the family behind. Never calling to talk, and rarely coming home. Relationships with siblings was strained, and being around her was awkward. She had fallen in love with someone who loved her with all his heart, but not her big family.

I grieved. Cried. Wept and wailed.

I woke up every day to a new day, but never in a new way. It was another day without her. The phone never rang. The ping of a much-needed text was silent. It just seemed that we were no longer important to her. We felt as if we had been discarded like a dirty dishrag. Being sucker punched by a loved one is exactly how that feels. The very ones we would take a bullet for can sometimes pull the trigger.

The feeling is indescribable.

The pain of betrayal is so deep and overcoming, it seems impossible. It is a hard kick in the gut that leaves us gasping for air. Breathless. There is a pit in the stomach that seems to open up and swallow one painful bite at a time. I got stuck in grief as if my feet were sinking in quicksand.

Being bitter is always scarred with trying to get even. Being better is always splattered and splashed with hope.

Those "heart-hurt" experiences of betrayal can make us either better or bitter. Being bitter is always scarred with trying to get even. Being better is always splattered and splashed with hope.

I made my choice. I chose to be bitter. Headaches, heartaches, and hard days lay ahead. I fell flat on my face and tripped over the trials of life. I shut the door on opportunities and opened the door to a bad thing named Bitter. I welcomed in and said hello to one of the ugliest enemies we can face as people—the enemy who steals joy, quiets laughter, smothers hope, ushers in loneliness, and gut punches the soul. Bitterness hardens the heart but disguises itself as strength. Don't be fooled. I knew if I chose bitterness over betterness, I would be sabotaged.

I woke up one morning, and I was done. Enough was enough! It was time to live again, trust again, and love without boundary lines.

I was face to face with backing up and starting over. How we back up determines how the rest of our life turns out. I had to start over. To get back in the race and run with arms wide open to the life that lay ahead. But most of all to never give up hope in a relationship being restored.

I had to stop walking around smelling like smoke from being burned. Come to the realization I also had blame, shame, and said things I could not take back. Once words are said, they can only be forgiven, not forgotten. It was time for me to take some responsibility too.

As a hardheaded, outspoken, southern woman, I learned God couldn't fix what I wouldn't face. So I faced it head-on. The truth is, I gave my opinion too much, and an opinion given without being asked for was criticism. My opinion used to make sense. Now it just gave offense.

My daughter didn't feel she could ever measure up to my expectations. I apologized with tears streaming down my cheeks. I wailed. I wept. I wanted her back as my daughter. However, me being in her life at this point was not something she was interested in. She could live without me in it. I had to make some tough choices.

Since the Lord is close to the brokenhearted and saves those who are crushed

> I could not
> control if she
> loved me or not.
> I had to face
> the cold hard
> fact: I had no
> control over
> anything except
> my own actions.

in spirit, I figured I qualified. I got out of the line of fire. I threw up the white flag of surrender.

I immersed myself in His Word. He pulled me up, lifted my chin, and assured me Jesus loved her more than I did. But most of all, He assured me I was lovable. I am still lovable. The words I so needed to know. The Bible is full of promises and comfort, and it was time I believed them for myself.

I could not control if she loved me or not. I had to face the cold hard fact: I had no control over anything except my own actions. It was time to pay attention to how I reacted from this day forward.

It was time to seek the sunshine again.

We all go through some kind of heart hurt and betrayal. From my experience I know it will steal your laughter, kill your joy, and try to destroy hope. The only anecdote for bitterness is forgiveness. Forgiveness is a strong-willed decision. However, it is the only decision that would bring me freedom from the prison of bitter bondage.

No more sitting, soaking, and souring. When we forgive and allow Jesus to heal our broken heart, he rearranges the letters in depression to spell "I pressed on."

Heart hurt can be hidden behind closed doors or out in the open. Want to live life fully alive? Laugh till your belly hurts and experience day-to-day joy? Then forgiveness is the only option. Unforgiveness will disqualify us. The price is way too high for unforgiveness. We must sell all of our stock in it now and press on.

Part of pressing on is to allow God to use someone to show us compassion. To be transparent and trust the one God sends.

*Compassion need not be complicated.* Comfort doesn't require big words or wise advice. Comfort for me was a friend's shoulder, crying till I could cry no more, and her petting my hair softly. There are times when "I am so sorry" is the best thing someone can say to someone who is hurting. And sometimes, when it's been a really tough week, it's all we need to hear.

When doubts filled my mind, your comfort gave me renewed hope and cheer. (Psalm 94:19 NLT)

*Father God,* show me how to love like You do. Show me how to express my deep, unconditional love in a way people can receive. Heal the places in my heart where I feel rejected and betrayed, and if bitterness is trying to build a wall, tear it down. I do not want to carry around anything in my heart that should not be there. I want freedom, forgiveness, and joy. Only You can set me free. Because of You I have hope that one day full restoration will happen because You tell me love never fails. In Jesus's name I pray. Amen.

Forgiveness is a strong-willed decision. However, it is the only decision that would bring me freedom from the prison of bitter bondage.

So here is the million-dollar question. How do we overcome bitterness when we've been betrayed, and truly forgive? When we seek Christ more than we seek revenge, He will unlock the prison door of bitterness. A life lived with bitterness is a life half lived. Jesus can put the heart back together when unforgiveness is ripping it apart.

Begin by trusting Jesus to do what He says He will do. He will come through. Everyone comes with some kind of baggage. Some of us pack bitterness. Other's negativity or perhaps anger. Jesus loves us enough to help us unpack. Here's a simple way you can begin the process:

1. Make a list of the bitterness that is causing you the most struggle.
2. Sit before Jesus and go over them one by one, praying and asking God to help you release the bitter events and hurts.
3. Shred or tear up the list as a symbol of letting go and allowing God to help you heal from the betrayal.

Tammy Whitehurst is a full-time speaker encouraging audiences to live life kicked up a notch. Her contagious joy will capture your heart. She is a former middle school teacher who struggles like the rest of us with life, cellulite, junk drawers, and wrinkles. Connect with her at TammyWhitehurst.com.

## Chapter Twenty-Six

# I Changed My Mind

### Jodi Harris

I wear betrayal like a thick wool blanket, heavy and suffocating, tripping over the dragging ends, unable to smoothly navigate it as I carry it through my day.

Most days I get ready, paste on a smile, and head out the door. Today's not that day.

Already past 10:00 a.m., I rise out of guilt, stumble to the coffeepot, not so much to wake to this new day before me but rather to reach out for liquid comfort, emotionally easing the tightness in my chest and jaw, aching from a long night of anxious dreams.

I stumble back to my bedroom, cradling my cup in my hands, breathing in warmth. I heave myself back into bed. My eyes close; my body fights gravity. I set the cup down, crawling back under covers to hide from this day, loud with sunlight, chirping birds, and clutter piles.

I poke my head out and now declare six more weeks of winter.

My emotions grow large and unmanageable. Sleep brings respite during this heartbreaking season I can't manage.

Recently the Enemy dug his claws deep into our church, where my husband pastors, and relentlessly attacked. Friends had betrayed us, making false accusations against my husband and his ministry, spreading lies to those who would lis-

What was it like
for Jesus when He
was betrayed by a
close friend?

ten. I struggled to make sense of these unfounded attacks, the slandering of their pastor, gossiping, and unwillingness to seek reconciliation.

I wanted to be above it all, unharmed, not letting the fiery arrows pierce my heart, but in the chaos and crossfire of the Enemy, I was deeply wounded. Church is a place I anticipate the love of Christ, His grace and mercy both given and received. What should have been the safest place on earth had become the most dangerous. I was ill prepared for the spiritual battle infiltrating our very walls and raging between Christ-followers.

And on this current day wrought with despondency, I confess that I didn't want to armor up and fight. I wanted to mope in misery. Linger longer in the pit of despair and amplify my agony. I'm dramatic like that. There was something satisfying about ruminating on the wrongs done to me and my husband, and entertaining thoughts of retaliation about our friends-turned-enemies. I relished in satisfaction over my dark plans for revenge.

I knew the Enemy was at work stealing my joy, tempting me with retaliation, and pounding lies into my head.

And I wondered, *What was it like for Jesus when He was betrayed by a close friend?* To be stabbed in the back? To experience heartache over the loss of a relationship with a fellow "believer" who'd walked closely with Him and the other disciples for three years? One He trusted to stand with Him when things got hard? And in the end, His friend Judas betrayed Him for thirty pieces of silver, the same amount paid for the life of an Israelite slave.

Or what was it like for David to be betrayed by King Saul? To be persecuted and falsely accused by someone he'd trusted?

I can relate to David when he laments in the psalms about multiple attacks against him. Words fall out from David's mouth that mirror my own:

> Malicious witnesses testify against me. They accuse me of crimes I know nothing about. They repay me evil for good. I am sick with despair. Yet when they were ill, I grieved for them. I denied myself

by fasting for them, but my prayers returned unanswered. I was sad, as though they were my friends or family, as if I were grieving for my own mother. But they are glad now that I am in trouble; they gleefully join together against me. I am attacked by people I don't even know; they slander me constantly. They mock me and call me names; they snarl at me. How long, O Lord, will you look on and do nothing? Rescue me from their fierce attacks. Protect my life from these lions! (Psalm 35:11–17 NLT)

*My thoughts exactly.*

One third of all the psalms are laments, passionate expressions of grief or sorrow. I return to read and study Psalm 35 to learn how David coped with betrayal, and I discover the answer in the psalms of lament.

Each psalm of lament contains the following six elements:

1. An address to God and a cry for help
2. A specific complaint
3. A confession of trust in God's power to deliver
4. A petition calling upon God to intervene
5. An assurance of being heard by God
6. A vow of praise and recognition that God is the only one capable of transforming the situation
   (A. C. Myers, *The Eerdmans Bible Dictionary* [Grand Rapids, MI: Eerdmans, 1987], 859.)

I'm pretty good at crying out to God for help and then complaining all over the place. I'm an expert at telling God how to handle my problem swiftly. I'm even certain He hears me. I have these parts nailed.

But then I let my mind wander and camp out in the deep hurts, wondering why I feel so bad. My time in the complaint department far outweighs my time in trust, gratitude, and praises to the very God who delivers and heals.

So I decide to change my thought process and practice lament like David. I take time to cry out to God, sharing with Him my pain and grief, just like David. I then transition my thoughts from my hurts to my Healer. I name truths about who God is and how He has worked in my life. I thank Him for hearing my prayer and praise Him for what He will do to redeem this situation and bring glory to His name.

I make a playlist of worship songs and play them on repeat during this season. I study the psalms and meditate on them.

Each time I'm tempted to fixate on what happened, I imperfectly practice lament, quicker to shift my thoughts from pain to praise. Quicker to dwell on the goodness of God and the gratitude I feel. My depression lessens. I find more peace. Practice doesn't make perfect, but hopefully it will make permanent.

My teenage son and husband arrive home one afternoon, and my son shares how they were driving through the canyon, when a car came at them head on, swerving out of the way at the last minute.

I ask him, "What did you do when you saw the car coming right at you? Did you panic?"

He responds, "I just looked at Dad."

Oh, how I want that immediate trust and confidence! When the trials of life are coming fast and furious, when I can't seem to catch a breath or a break, may my first instinct be to look at my heavenly Abba, Father.

In their book *The Songs of Jesus*, Timothy and Kathy Keller say, "Lord, believing the promise of Your presence in my suffering takes time, and grows slowly, through stages in prayer. So, I will pray until my heart rejoices in you. Amen" (Viking, 2015).

*I will pray until my heart rejoices in You!*

I am not excluded from His transforming power through praise. God chooses to use my story to reveal His glory. And He will use yours.

In this season of painful betrayal, I will pray until my heart rejoices in God. Until my first response to suffering is fixing my eyes on Jesus and dwelling in His presence. Until people ask, "What's different about you?"

And I can say, "I changed my mind."

In this season of painful betrayal, I will pray until my heart rejoices in God.

You will keep in perfect peace all who trust in you, all whose thoughts are fixed on you! (Isaiah 26:3 NLT)

Don't copy the behavior and customs of this world, but let God transform you into a new person by changing the way you think. Then you will learn to know God's will for you, which is good and pleasing and perfect. (Romans 12:2)

Don't worry about anything; instead, pray about everything. Tell God what you need, and thank him for all he has done. Then you will experience God's peace, which exceeds anything we can understand. His peace will guard your hearts and minds as you live in Christ Jesus.

And now, dear brothers and sisters, one final thing. Fix your thoughts on what is true, and honorable, and right, and pure, and lovely, and admirable. Think about things that are excellent and worthy of praise. Keep putting into practice all you learned and received from me—everything you heard from me and saw me doing. Then the God of peace will be with you. (Philippians 4:6-9 NLT)

~ Resilient Prayer

*Lord*, help my first response in times of betrayal be to turn to You. As I pour out my heart and hurt, may I also proclaim the truths of who You are, what You have done, and what You will do. You are a friend who sticks closer than a brother (Proverbs 18:24). You love me with an unfailing love and will never let me go. In Jesus's name. Amen.

 *Resilient Action*

Read Psalm 35. In the space below, write your own lament about a current painful situation based on the six elements.

1. An address to God and a cry for help
2. A specific complaint
3. A confession of trust in God's power to deliver
4. A petition calling upon God to intervene
5. An assurance of being heard by God
6. A vow of praise and recognition that God is the only one capable of transforming the situation

As a Bible teacher, speaker, and writer, Jodi Harris is in passionate pursuit of Jesus and living a better story. She is contributing author to the books *Bloom Where You're Planted: Stories of Women in Church Planting, Volumes 1, 2, and 3.* Connect with her at justjodiharris.com, where she writes about life and struggles, Scripture, and the importance of coffee creamer.

## Chapter Twenty-Seven

## The Morning After
### Liz Tate

A cataclysmic storm has just hit your place of residence. It has sent you in a whirlwind, and you can't believe it's actually happening. When you woke up on this day, you were reflecting back on how you just loved the calmness and serenity that each day brings from your still new-to-you country living.

Calm? Serene? Will I ever experience it again? The news was like a Category 5 hurricane hitting home in full force, and nothing will ever be the same.

There was no newsflash or any indicators or warnings to even let me know a storm was brewing. Nothing! It hit so unexpectedly and left me raw with emotions, full of fury, and questioning why.

As I stretched out on the floor—in what I like to call my secret place, really my office—all I could do was scream. And I do mean *scream*. As I cried out, I grew numb from utter exhaustion. I felt like winter had come without notice. It was as if I were lying there and was frozen stiff. I had just learned some upsetting news. Every time I recalled the news, it sent chills up and down my spine.

"Fret not yourself because of evildoers; be not envious of wrongdoers! For they will soon fade like the grass and whither like the green herb" (Psalm 37:1 ESV).

Hurt is pumping all through my veins. My heart aching from the pain of the news. My flesh desperately wanting vengeance. Oh, how I am consoled by this promise from the first verse of Psalm 37.

And then I read on.

"Trust in the Lord, and do good" (v. 3).

Oh, Lord God, please forgive me for all the wicked thoughts that are plaguing my mind. There is no good that can come from them. This news threatens to consume me, and I just don't know how I will go on.

The question that I continue to ask myself is, "Will I ever make it through *the Morning After*?"

Days and days go by as the storm ravages my soul. I have days that are quite chilly, and I experience prayers dry and cold, with no life or heart in them. I have rainy days where the tears just will not end, going from sun up to sun down and all through the midnight hour. Along with the rain are gale-force winds blowing me emotionally to and fro. And yes, there are a few sunny days where I feel the warm presence of my Savior Jesus. Son shine! Son shine! Son shine!

*This. Just. Is. Not. Fair.* These five words, strung together in pause, become my mantra.

A child? As a result of adultery? And to hide it from me for over five years? He said he couldn't have children. It was the hidden desire of his heart, Lord, and I know you knew this. This is his reward for the ultimate betrayal? And I will have to somehow live with the remnant of his unspoken deception? In my face? As a constant reminder of the humiliation?

*This. Just. Is. Not. Fair.*

## Survival and Preparation

The storm was interesting because, as mentioned, not only did it hit unexpectedly but with it brought a new season of life. A season where survival was truly a matter of life or death.

> Oh, Lord, how long will you forget me? Forever? How long will you look the other way?

How long must I struggle with anguish in my soul, with sorrow in my heart every day?

How long will my enemy have the upper hand?

Trust and answer me, O Lord my God! Restore the sparkle to my eyes, or I will die.

Don't let my enemies gloat, saying, "We have defeated him!" Don't let them rejoice at my downfall.

But I trust in your unfailing love. I will rejoice because You have rescued me.

I will sing to the Lord because He is good to me. (Psalm 13 NLT)

In Psalm 13 David is brutally honest with himself and with God. So if that meant in the midst of his despair and frustration, he goes from impatience, to a cry for help, and then to praise, then so be it. That was his heart. David trusted God.

So maybe . . . just maybe God is okay with questions and honest-to-God heartfelt expressions. The what is really on your mind and in your heart type. In every season. Maybe God wants to hear songs and prayers that pour out from us expressing our honest feelings and true emotions reflective of a dynamic and life-changing *friendship* with Him. Because we trust Him. Even in the times when it doesn't seem fair. I do believe this is what David knew.

In Jeremiah 12, Jeremiah is personally struggling with life, and he just doesn't understand why things happen the way they do. Jeremiah brought his questions to God in this season of his life too. Interesting questions. Just how-he-felt-at-the-moment questions. Questions like why do the wicked prosper? Why are all they who deal very treacherously and deceitfully at ease and thriving?

You know what? In this passage God answers Jeremiah: "If you have raced with men on foot, and they have wearied you, how will you compete with horses?" (Jeremiah 12:17 ESV).

Maybe God wants to hear songs and prayers that pour out from us expressing our honest feelings and true emotions reflective of a dynamic and life-changing friendship with Him.

The Light of the world is shining down on us. No matter where we are in this journey, our race, He is shining down on us.

This is probably not the answer Jeremiah was expecting. Girl, me either!

Oh, but it was in this answer that I was able to press on. It was in this answer that the Holy Spirit spoke words of strength and encouragement.

Don't let the storm tire you out. Run your race. This is only the beginning. God has so much more for you, and this is all to prepare you for what is to come. You want to live in a land of security where you are not stretched and made to be totally dependent on Him? *Really?* Then how will He prepare you for what is to come? He knows. He's got this. Have faith in Him. Trust Him.

There was a day I looked up at the sky, which was painted like a mural. It was one of the initial days of walking through the aftermath of my storm. The moon was lightning white. Just a crescent moon, but it was positioned like a smile. That seemed odd to me because although I have seen many crescent moons, I could not remember ever seeing the moon quite like this. All I could think about as my husband drove and I looked up at the heavens was Jesus. The Light of the world is shining down on us. No matter where we are in this journey, our race, He is shining down on us.

Hebrews 12 (NIV) starts out with this:

> Therefore, since we are surrounded by so great a cloud of witnesses, let us throw off everything that hinders and the sin that so easily entangles. And let us run with perseverance the race marked out for us, fixing our eyes on Jesus, the pioneer and perfecter of our faith. For the joy set before him he endured the cross, scorning its shame, and sat down at the right hand of the throne of God. Consider him who endured such opposition from sinners, so that you will not grow weary and lose heart.

My sista, I think every day we face life or death. Life is when we choose to live our lives patterned after Christ. Death is when we choose to yield to the human reasoning of the soul with no help from above. Choose life. Be determined to stay on this journey choosing life, and see every moment (even stormy ones) as an opportunity to grow and trust God more and more each and every day.

## Resilient Truth

In You, O Lord, do I put my trust and seek refuge; let me never be put to shame or [have my hope in You] disappointed; deliver me in Your righteousness! (Psalm 31:1 AMPC)

## Resilient Prayer

*Father*, there are days where I just cannot seem to move forward. I want justice now. I want this all to go away. I don't think it's fair. In the days where the hurt threatens to consume me, help me to remember this: You are good and You are faithful. Help me to trust in Your way. For You to have Your way in the whirlwind and in the storm. In Jesus's name. Amen.

Life is when we choose to live our lives patterned after Christ. Death is when we choose to yield to the human reasoning of the soul with no help from above. Choose life.

Write down your innermost feeling and thoughts related to the marriage betrayal as if you were communicating to your best friend. Be open and honest about how you feel with yourself. Also, find a Scripture promise that encourages you to press on and trust God.

Take what you wrote down to God. Talk. Scream. Cry. Let it out. At the end of your conversation, speak the Scripture promise over your life and praise God for His faithfulness and goodness.

Plan to repeat the action as often as necessary.

Liz Tate is a writer with a vision to strengthen and encourage women across the globe to reach their full potential, with a mission to glorify God. Liz wants to see women transformed to be all that God has called them to be. You can find her at www.Ezra728.org, Instagram, and Facebook.

## Chapter Twenty-Eight

### Prisoner of Hope
#### Sheri Hawley

I sat down in the chair near my handsome young husband, who was almost ready to leave. Neither of us spoke. The house was silent as predawn light pushed in at the windows. He smelled of my favorite cologne. I hugged my knees to my chest and finally said, "You're having an affair, aren't you."

My voice was flat and devoid of emotion. I looked up, waiting silently for his response to what was meant more as a statement than a question. The vivid dream that had just awakened me had already answered all my questions. Explicit in detail, the dream rocked me to my core and had the ominous feel of a warning. It revealed what I hadn't dared to consider. Frank was having an affair, and everyone around us knew it except me.

Waiting for his response, I thought back on what had brought us to this moment. Frank and I, married almost ten years, had three beautiful little girls just five years apart in age. We lived far from any family, so we had no extra hands to help. Since most nights were spent comforting one or more of the girls who couldn't sleep, I was perpetually exhausted.

Frank's job demanded a lot of extra hours but offered no overtime pay. Our meager finances had become a constant source of stress and disagreement. Frank and I loved one another, but over the previous two years, things had changed. He had turned his attention toward his fast-paced successful career, and I (a former teacher) had chosen to focus on getting through every day as a stay-at-home mom.

Our conversations now revolved around just three topics: the girls, his work, and our finances. The last two seemed to always lead to a major argument, so we eventually avoided anything beyond asking how the day had gone for each other.

Since Frank's office was only ten minutes from home, I insisted he at least be with us for dinner each evening. While he agreed that was important, there always seemed to be some meeting or left-over assignment urgently requiring his attention. He would eat quickly, kiss us each goodbye, and then dash back out the door, not returning until long after the girls were in bed. To help ease our financial struggle, he took on a part-time job for two days each week. Our situation went from bad to worse.

I was quickly brought back to the present by the look of utter shock on Frank's face and his adamant words declaring he had no idea what I was talking about. "Sheri, why would you even say something like that? No, I'm not having an affair!"

I knew in my heart he must be telling the truth, but I remained resolute. "Then what was that dream about?" We weren't big believers in every dream having meaning, but there had been two others like this one that had held great significance for us. Frank remembered them, and so did I.

He straightened his tie, then picked up his coat to leave. "We'll talk about it this afternoon."

It never occurred to either of us that he should take a personal day so we could talk right then about what was wrong. You see, it was Sunday, and he was a pastor.

## A Common Struggle

Our story was just like those of so many others. We eventually learned Frank *was* having an affair, but it wasn't with another woman. No, the true object of his affection was his work. Like other young men his age, work had become his key source of affirmation and identity. He became less and less engaged with the family he loved because he was drawn to the siren call of his work.

"I'm doing this for *us*" was his usual response when I would question his long hours. I continued to wrestle with all the feelings associated with most marriage betrayals: sorrow, loneliness, loss, unworthiness, and even rage, but none was as intense as my feelings of guilt.

> We excuse ourselves from taking action because we don't want to impugn our character or that of our spouse.

When a man "abandons" his wife for his job, she must also deal with many unexpected questions: "How could you be so selfish?" "What more do you want from this man?" "He's a hard worker! Stop being so demanding." "Get yourself together. It will eventually get better."

In our early years, I had been warned to protect my marriage from the opposite sex. But from his work? From our church? I had no idea how to move forward. It was clear that the children and I did not have a place of priority in his heart. Each new project he took on, every time he came in from the office with no emotional reserves left for us, proved that my husband had another he loved more.

We determined something had to be done. Divorce was never discussed, but we realized we were moving into a dangerous mode of apathy. Neither of us wanted to settle for the mediocre marriage we saw others accepting. So we made plans to travel to a Christian counseling agency that focused on pastoral marriages. Our weeklong experience provided a major turning point.

## There Is Hope

Glen, our counselor, knew all about the shroud of embarrassment and silence that forces many couples to never seek help. He said we excuse ourselves from taking action because we don't want to impugn our character or that of our spouse. Sometimes we don't want to "own" our unhealthy expectations of marriage. He quickly identified key issues Frank and I had used to lock ourselves into a place with no escape.

Control topped our list. Frank and I were both firstborn children, and we always had our own plan for every situation. Those plans seldom intersected. Glen helped us to better appreciate the ideas we each brought to the table. He urged both of us to expose our hidden desires to control the other. It was first humbling and then healing to confess these things to one another.

Glen also addressed the fact that we had no *grace* working in our marriage. Frank and I approached every argument as the offended party, never acknowledging the pain our own words caused. Glen challenged us to wipe the slate clean, to forgive, and to start asking the Holy Spirit to bring grace into our thoughts, words, and actions. We accepted the simple yet profound truth that we are *all* broken and we *all* need a Savior.

Frank and I realigned our priorities, assigning God first place, our spouse second, our children third, and our work fourth. We took our tears to the Father, and He used them to soften the soil of our hearts toward one another. We began using the communication tools provided through counseling to plant seeds of hope and joy. Eventually we saw the budding of new fruit.

I started being more intentional about monitoring my thought life. I focused on why I had loved Frank in the first place. I rehearsed his good qualities to myself, to our daughters, and to my friends. I stopped nagging.

Frank planned a better budget, and we worked together to get out of debt. He chose to be home with us more. He prayed with me. He maintained contact with our counselor for check-up calls.

Months later Frank led us in taking a truly drastic step toward emotional health. We left the large church we both loved and moved across the state, taking on a pioneer work with only thirteen parishioners. That bold action recalibrated our lives.

We're still broken, and we still need a Savior daily, but our three girls grew up knowing they were loved and that they could trust God for every part of their journey. They now serve Christ with their

> We had no grace working in our marriage. Frank and I approached every argument as the offended party, never acknowledging the pain our own words caused.

own dedicated husbands and have given us nine practically perfect grandchildren.

A happy marriage is the union of two good forgivers.

Ruth Bell Graham said, "A happy marriage is the union of two good forgivers" (ChristianCenteredMama.com). Perhaps you, too, are in a place of desperation, experiencing the pain of a disappointing marriage relationship. I urge you to start with grace and forgiveness. Pray for these characteristics to increase in your own life. Then ask God to make you a "prisoner of hope," as described in Zechariah 9:12, where God promises that he will restore twice as much to you. A marriage that's twice as healthy as you ever thought possible? It's totally possible!

## Resilient Truth

Let us then approach the throne of grace with confidence, so that we may receive mercy and find grace to help us in our time of need. (Hebrews 4:16)

## Resilient Prayer

*Heavenly Father,* it feels like none of the dreams from my wedding day are being fulfilled—our marriage isn't what I expected. Perhaps my ideals weren't as healthy as they should be. Forgive me for my part in our marriage struggles. Help me turn over to You all the things I want to control. Let my brokenness become the very place where You can plant a heathier perspective. May I walk in grace toward my partner and lean on You, Holy Spirit, for the grace and mercy we need to move forward. As I allow You to change me, may my spouse also be prompted to respond to You, Holy Spirit. Let us boldly recalibrate to give You first place and to become an example of Your love for our family and the world. In Jesus's name. Amen.

 *Resilient Action*

Is your family relationship properly aligned? Begin to pray aloud, asking God to make you a prisoner of hope regarding your marriage. Make a list of Bible verses that speak to your heart about grace and forgiveness. If needed, reach out to a Christian counselor for help.

Sheri Hawley is a writer, speaker, ordained pastor, and noni. Her work has appeared in multiple publications, including *Faith and Freedom* and *Just Between Us Magazine*. You can find her at sherihawley.com (Embrace the Grace), and on Facebook.

## Chapter Twenty-Nine

## Betrayed by Others, Beloved by God
### Kennita Williams

Betrayal, it's an emotional letdown that we have all experienced on some level. Being betrayed can feel like a roller coaster of feelings—it's painful and can cause us to not trust and leave us feeling empty.

Betrayal by a loved one or a close friend can leave you angry, depressed, and often confused. How can someone love me one moment and betray me the next? I have been faced with these feelings more than I would like to admit. Betrayal became so frequent in my life that one day I found myself making a vow that I would not allow betrayal to darken my doorstep again. As a military spouse, I was given the opportunity to put this vow into action.

After twelve years of being stationed in Florida, my husband came home one day and announced we had been given a special assignment to Alaska. To his surprise, I accepted the news with gladness. I knew this was my chance to do things differently, that this was my chance to meet new people and never allow myself to be betrayed again. This time would be different. I would do everything in my power to rise above betrayal.

We packed our things and journeyed to our new venture. For months I had decided to introduce myself, not say too much, not do too much. We joined a new church, and immediately my husband and children got involved, but not me. I just came in, took a seat, and wore a smile.

This time I wanted things to be different—getting involved would not get me this time. I refused to get hurt and disappointed . . . it wouldn't happen again. I continued this pattern for months.

Then one Wednesday evening I arrived at the chapel to pick up my daughter from youth group, and she invited her adviser to the car to meet me. This young lady said that my daughter had mentioned I was the women's director in my previous church. I responded with a yes, and immediately I wanted to take it back, but it was too late. The secret was out, and before I knew it, I had agreed to meet about starting a women's group at the chapel.

I thought, *Lord, what have I done? How have I found myself back in such a place?*

I took a deep breath and reminded myself of the vow I'd made months before. *This time will be different. This is a different group. I am in a different location. These ladies all have a common goal. We are all leaders that want to bless God's people and build the kingdom.* These were the words I found myself repeating over and over again while looking in the mirror.

I decided to forget about the past and get back to doing what I knew God had called me to do. Work in women's ministry. I went to the meeting and immediately got to work, gave ideas to set up the program from paper to reality. Everything went well, women were involved, and the group grew.

One day I came to a meeting, and positions had been given, and I quickly realized it was happening again. The table I'd created had been given to another conductor, and I was the last to know. After weeks of asking why and searching for answers, I was greeted by new leadership to say, "We have decided to go another way."

How could this be?

*This cannot be happening again.* Betrayal. The ugly word showed up again. On came the hurt, followed by disappointment, but this time I decided I was not going to let this happen again.

I was not going to let betrayal win.

I was going to move forward.

The same thing had happened to me. How could I make it different? I had to fight with a different weapon.

I was going to handle this differently.

I had to take it to the Lord. I'd moved to a new location, I'd sat at a different table, but yet the same thing had happened to me. How could I make it different? I had to fight with a different weapon.

I was reminded of David in Psalm 55:1–8, 12–23. David was betrayed by someone close to him. This is how the Enemy tries to defeat us; the hurt comes from the ones we least expect. David was hurt, but instead of handling it the wrong way through anger or a devious plan of revenge, he went to the Lord about it. He expressed himself. He was real and transparent about how it made him feel. David trusted in God's ability and left it in God's capable hands to work it out for him.

By doing it David's way, I gained the strength to move forward. I learned when dealing with betrayal we can be like David and bring our thoughts and emotions to the Lord. If we are going to overcome betrayal, we need to leave the matter at His feet and let Him deal with it and the people who have betrayed us (1 Peter 5:17).

## Resilient Truth

If you forgive those who sin against you, your heavenly Father will forgive you. But if you refuse to forgive others, your Father will not forgive your sins. (Matthew 6:14–15 NLT)

## Resilient Prayer

*Lord*, I trust You. I have been hurt, I have been betrayed, but I trust You. Help me to move forward with other relationships. Help me to not punish, by assuming they will be like the people in my past, those who mean me no harm. Help me to rebuild trust in the ones who hurt me, if it be Your will to reconcile with them. Give me the grace to follow the process and trust You to make all things new.

 Resilient Action

Take some time to answer these questions:

1. Why is it important to take your betrayal to the Lord?
2. How does David's way of overcoming betrayal help control our thoughts and emotions?
3. List the benefits of trusting the Lord with our betrayal.

Kennita Williams is military spouse, mother of two, and a certified life coach. She has walked a path from not seeing a clear vision to knowing God's purpose for her life. Through her writing, she encourages women to be all God has planned for them to be. She's also a victim's advocate, and she serves as a US Air Force legal assistant. She lives in North Pole, Alaska. Connect with Kennita on Facebook and Instagram.

## Chapter Thirty

## Dare to Forgive
### Cynthia Cavanaugh

I was headed to the local cafe and had planned to do some journaling and reflecting. I noticed an elderly woman sitting in the next booth all by herself. I had an overwhelming urge to invite her to have lunch with me. It wouldn't go away. When God whispers, He is insistent. I argued with God this was my time, and I didn't really want to talk to anybody. He wouldn't leave me alone, and so wanting to be obedient, I asked her if she wanted to join me for lunch. She gave a resounding *yes*, and I cringed inwardly. *Okay, God, this better be good!*

As we ate, she began to tell me her story. She had been in church all her life and been woefully betrayed. I empathized with her, but the bitterness of unforgiveness oozed like a poison in her words. Her heart appeared tainted by her inability to forgive. God gave me a strong warning in my soul and whispered to me that if I couldn't let go, lean in, and trust Him with forgiving, I too would end up like this woman.

This realization scared me to death. It was like looking into my future thirty years down the road. I left that day shaken by what God showed me and slid into my car. I told God I needed his help to fully work through forgiving those who had wounded me. It was a defining moment, and whenever I am tempted to hold on to the pain of unforgiveness, I remember that day at the local café.

You see, months earlier I had been working through gut-wrenching betrayal. I experienced verbal wounding and spiritual abuse in both my marriage and church leadership, all of which sent me into a dizzying spin of confusion, and I began to question what I had believed my whole life. I went into a full-fledged ICU treatment, so to speak, and began to unravel thirty-five-plus years of unhealthy thinking and relating.

I have mostly considered myself a forgiving person. Trying to live by a value not to hold grudges and keep short accounts for the most part has served me well. And yet within a period of years this core value was put through a scorching fire. Although this chapter will not allow me to share all the story that led to my greatest forgiveness challenge, I will say this—my greatest fear in life has been the fear of feeling misunderstood.

I give myself 150 percent in relationships with others and love getting to the heart of the matter with friends and family. When relationships don't work, I sometimes try too hard, and it gets me in trouble. I try to take on more in the relationship than is healthy. I think counselors call this codependency—in other words, taking on feeling responsible for other people's happiness. It is a family-of-origin curse that my sister and I laugh about sometimes as we try to detangle ourselves from this unhealthy behavior.

Because this was my pattern, it brought me to a perfect storm, and what I mean by a perfect storm is that several different aspects and transitions in life collided at the same time, and I was unprepared for the events and reactions. If ever I was misunderstood, this was the quintessential moment in my life.

As I unraveled my unhealthiness both emotionally and spiritually, I realized that I wasn't really *that good* at forgiving. You see, forgiveness is easier, and I say this cautiously, when things are resolved. But the biggest challenge for me in forgiving is when there is no resolve on the horizon. When you try so desperately to be understood, and there still is no resolve. That is the toughest piece of forgiveness to practice. And this is what scared me to death with the encounter at the local café. I didn't want my lack of forgiveness to transform me into a bitter, cranky old woman.

There is a powerful principle of forgiveness in the story of Luke when Jesus has dinner at the home of a Pharisee. When a woman came in and began washing Jesus's feet, the Pharisee was surprised Jesus would let this woman touch Him. The Pharisee knew her reputation. If Jesus was who He said He was, He would know her reputation too, and He certainly wouldn't have let this unclean woman touch him. But Jesus knew this Pharisee's thoughts:

> Then he turned to the woman and said to Simon, "Look at this woman kneeling here. When I entered your home, you didn't offer me water to wash the dust from my feet, but she has washed them with her tears and wiped them with her hair. You didn't greet me with a kiss, but from the time I first came in, she has not stopped kissing my feet. You neglected the courtesy of olive oil to anoint my head, but she has anointed my feet with rare perfume. I tell you, her sins—and they are many—have been forgiven, so she has shown me much love. But a person who is forgiven little shows only little love." Then Jesus said to the woman, "Your sins are forgiven." The men at the table said among themselves, "Who is this man, that he goes around forgiving sins?" And Jesus said to the woman, "Your faith has saved you; go in peace." (Luke 7:44–50 NLT)

Most of the time this passage is referred to in a teaching session as a passage about what it means to worship. As I studied this, God gave me new eyes to see the heart of this story—it's not just about giving my all to Jesus in worship, as Mary did, but it is a story about forgiveness and my willingness to love much because I've been forgiven much.

If we don't choose to forgive, our influence will be locked up. It will be a life sentence of misery. We will lose our special assignment of influence. The profound words of Jesus in this story to the Pharisee, who is judging Mary for her act of worship, is in what Jesus says: "But a

It is a story about forgiveness and my willingness to love much because I've been forgiven much.

We can't possibly love others with a full heart if we can't dare to forgive.

person who is forgiven little shows only little love"! In other words, what Jesus is communicating to us is that we can't possibly love others with a full heart if we can't dare to forgive the ones who have hurt us, betrayed us, and misunderstood us.

If you have been alive long enough, you will be betrayed and wounded. I am not telling you anything you don't already know. When we are brutally betrayed, we can be tempted to hang on to the hurt and feel exempt from forgiving. The Bible speaks otherwise. Let's take a refresher course on what the Bible says about forgiveness:

Matthew 18:21—"How often do I forgive?" Peter asked. Seventy times seven.
Luke 17:3–5—We can't forgive on our own. We need God's help.
Colossians 3:13—As the Lord has forgiven me, I must also forgive.
Matthew 6:14—If we don't forgive, God will not forgive us. Ouch!

So what does this mean, you say, in the light of betrayal we can't seem to get over? I can't answer for you, only for me. Only you can provide the answer, and it is between you and God, and hopefully with the help of skilled counselors. I wouldn't dare to prescribe a formula of what forgiveness looks like for reconciliation. Each situation is different.

I do know this one staunch truth: we are called and commanded to forgive.

It is the greatest gift we can give ourselves, and we can give grace to others. But the healing journey of reconciliation is a delicate process.

I have found myself over and over again asking, but what does this mean for me? It is complicated. I won't pretend it is easy. Sometimes we are asked to walk a hard road of forgiveness and reconciliation. But remember not to confuse trust with forgiveness, and don't allow distrust to keep you from forgiving. God doesn't ask us to trust a person who has betrayed us immediately. Forgiveness is a process. We are called to forgive so our hearts remain pure and no weed of bitterness takes root. Don't wait. Do it now while the conviction is hovering over your heart. Don't let the temptation of the tempest of unforgiveness steal your future and cause you to become like the bitter-filled woman at the café.

Put on then, as God's chosen ones, holy and beloved, compassionate hearts, kindness, humility, meekness, and patience, bearing with one another and, if one has a complaint against another, forgiving each other; as the Lord has forgiven you, so you also must forgive. And above all these put on love, which binds everything together in perfect harmony. (Colossians 3:12–14 ESV)

～ *Resilient Prayer*

*Jesus,* my heart is aching with the pain of betrayal and hurt. I can't forgive on my own. It's too hard. Help me to let go and release the wound so I won't become bitter. Thank You for Your mercy and forgiveness. Because You have forgiven me, I ask You for the strength to forgive. In Jesus's name. Amen.

Don't allow
distrust to
keep you from
forgiving.

*Resilient Action*

Find a quiet place for thirty minutes to answer the following questions:

- What do you need to let go of and let God handle for reconciliation? Whom do you need to release in surrender to the one who promises He will take care of it? (Make a list.)
- Stop and pray for the people you need to forgive, and ask God to help you trust Him if there is never any resolution.
- Now tear up your list, offer it to God as your first step, and acknowledge your need to forgive.

Cynthia Cavanaugh is a speaker, life coach, and award-winning author of *Anchored: Leading through the Storms* and *Live Bold: A Devotional Journal to Strengthen Your Soul*. She is the strategic marketing coach for Redemption Press, and you can find her at www.cynthiacavanaugh.com, Facebook, and Instagram, and her new podcast, *Soul Anchor*.

# Copyrights

Ordering

*She Writes for Him*

ROMANS 8:28
BOOKS
AN IMPRINT OF REDEMPTION
PRESS

**To order additional copies of this book, please visit**
www.redemption-press.com.
Also available on Amazon.com
Or by calling toll free 1-844-2REDEEM.